Gags and Greasepaint

Gags and Greasepaint:
A Tribute to the Irish "Fit-Ups"

792. 29417

By

Vikki Jackson

Edited by Mícheál Ó hAodha

Cambridge Scholars Publishing

Gags and Greasepaint: A Tribute to the Irish "Fit-Ups",
by Vikki Jackson (Edited by Mícheál Ó hAodha)

This book first published 2008 by

Cambridge Scholars Publishing

15 Angerton Gardens, Newcastle, NE5 2JA, UK

British Library Cataloguing in Publication Data
A catalogue record for this book is available from the British Library

ISBN (10): 1-84718-510-X, ISBN (13): 9781847185105

TABLE OF CONTENTS

OPENING CHORUS

I would like this book to be a tribute to the women and men of the "Fit-Ups", those brave troubadours who entertained in villages and towns the length and breadth of Ireland, to the showpeople who brought smiles and happiness to many a poor and joyless village and town in the era before and after the Second World. The "Fit-Ups" wasn't just a game to these show people. It was their living and it was hard work, although hardly a day went by when there wasn't somebody up to some ruse or prank that brought fun to the whole troupe. The Showpeople, referred to on occasion as members of the "touring class" were a unique people, "a people apart" who spent their lives on-stage because of their love of it. The travelling and the "road-life" was difficult. Let's not romantise all of that. The negotiations in advance, the hanging of bills, the learning of scripts and preparing of costumes and scenery. Then there was the setting up, the search for 'digs', and then the live evening performances before audiences that were far more discerning than people today might often consider. They were entertaining pre-television audiences - whether in the smallest village or the largest town - audiences who had come to see the 'play actors' and knew a "good show" from a bad one. They entertained a fussy lot and rightly so! – an audience who would let you know in no uncertain terms whether you were good or bad! To write the definitive work on the Fit-ups would be an impossible task given that so many records have been lost or were never committed to paper in the first place. The Showpeople's tradition was to a large degree an oral tradition handed on from family to family – father to son, mother to daughter. Posters were frequently discarded, photographs not always available or affordable! - and family histories never recorded. Much of this book depends on people's memories, some good, some bad, - but never, ever dull!!

Vikki Jackson,
Bruree, County Limerick.
January, 2007

PROLOGUE

This book is a paean to the "Fit-Ups". It is a celebration of the "curtain up", and the "five-and-nine". It is a hymn to the "gods and goddesses" of the road show and the repertory. It is our way of paying homage to those heroes and heroines who came before us and who braved wind, rain and the vagaries of the road. These brave souls transported us and elevated the senses. Theirs was the magic of disguise, innovation and song. Many was the dull hall and damp outhouse they transformed through hard work, imagination and the joy of the dramatic moment. Glitz, glamour, and the vibrant excitement of scenery, prop and the forgotten magic that is the play of light. Costumes to make the heart sing and the Sequin Queen! Many was the country imagination that Vic Loving and her contemporaries initiated into the unique and wondrous magic of theatre and song. Many was the crowd that roared, hissed, booed and laughed with an exuberance that the "box in the corner" (F.N) will never equal!! Ireland is changed beyond recognition but the old voices still cry out from where they lie hidden in the excitement and magic of the stage-wings, the garish display of paint-glow and the tread of the footboard. Listen up because this is one "one last hurrah" to the performers of yesteryear, to Vic Loving – the Sequin Queen – and to the hearts that were never the same afterwards.

Dr. Mícheál Ó hAodha,
Department of History
University of Limerick, Ireland.

ACKNOWLEDGEMENTS

There are some people I want to thank for getting me to use my "little grey cells" to get this book on the road...

Initially, the late Ted O'Riordan of Charleville, County Cork asked me to write an article on Granny Vic. That was a long time ago, but it set the ball rolling. Some more writing of articles followed which jogged people's memories of the shows, which in turn jogged my memory of forgotten stories of my "growing up" years. The talks on radio and TV brought sackfuls of letters (thanks Austin) from people far and near all wanting to share memories - *Thank you.*

To others who came to Briar Cottage to do research of the shows relevant to the counties they came from. Many thanks to Joe Carroll, Pat Tuohy, Paddy Buckley, Andy Tobin, Pat Houlihan, Tom O'Donnell, Kieran Fitzgerald, Mike McGrath, Christopher Roche, Jenny O'Sullivan, Janet Murphy, Ciara Farrell, Nancy Leahy – and to all the other names too numerous to mention - but which are in my visitor's book.

To Mícheál for taking this on-board and trying to decipher my scribblings!

Thanks for all of your memories and keeping alive those far off but not forgotten days.

Vic Loving and son Chic in 1927

Vic Loving and son Chic c. 1940

Front view of Vic Loving's Show

Vic Loving's Dancing troupe perform an acrobatic feat

THERE'S NO BUSINESS LIKE SHOW-BUSINESS

'Fit-ups' was a term used to describe the travelling road show and theatrical companies which once toured Ireland. The scenery which 'fitted' together; the large tents and marquees slotted and joined to create another world where audiences could lose themselves in a fantasy of beautiful costumes, sets, variety and drama. The days of the travelling shows are long since gone, other forms of entertainment having replaced them. Gone too are the days when people young and old walked, sometimes for miles, to see the 'actors' who made them laugh, cry, boo, cheer and clap at the plays, good, and not so good. Entertainers of all kinds; singers, dancers, comedians, magicians, acrobats. For sheer good value it was hard to beat the 'Fit-ups'. Indeed they spawned many a local amateur dramatic or musical group, spurred on by the 'glamour of the footlights'

There have always been travelling shows: groups of troubadours going from village to village, town to town, and all points in between. But it was in Ireland that they flourished.

One of the earliest companies was "The Bohemians", owned by Tommy Conway who had joined Barry's Circus at an early age thus giving the young Tommy a taste for the stage. Later he went into Music Hall, touring both England and Ireland, and formed his own travelling show in the late 1800s. A highly talented man, he wrote his own sketches and monologues, performed acrobatics, and was also a dab hand at painting scenery. By all accounts he was an excellent boss. He is best remembered for his prolific songwriting including, amongst others, "The Moonshiner" and "HelloPatsy Fagin". Talent indeed....!!

It was between the 1920s and late 1960s that the road shows thrived. There were over eighty of them, at one stage, criss-crossing Ireland, from the well-established to those which lasted no more then a few months. Of course people from different shows joined other companies, getting to know a lot of other 'pros'. It was like a rather large family.The 'Fit-ups' were to Ireland what The End of the Pier' shows were to England. Names to come out of seaside entertainment included Leslie Crowther, Arthur Askey, Merle Oberon, G.H.Elliot and Tony Hancock to name but a few.

However the names to emerge from the 'Fit-ups' were equally famous: Cyril Cusack, Anna Managhan, Hal Roach, Milo O'Shea, Barry Cassin, Bob Carrickford, Sandy Kelly. In England a lot of 'wandering minstrels' from the seaside shows went into Music Hall. They too were very successful, but the Music Hall lost some of its best artistes who left to form their own companies in Ireland. One of these artistes was Vic Loving

THE SEQUIN QUEEN:
THE STORY OF VIC LOVING

Vic Loving was born in 1890 in Madrid, Spain to a Spanish mother and a Welsh father. Her passport states her birthplace as Manchester, England, and she lived there since her parents, who had run a circus in Europe, moved to Lancashire. Her father had opened a butcher's shop where he ran a thriving business but given her background it was natural for Vic to want to go into the entertainment business. So, as a youngster, she and a childhood friend (one Gracie Fields) sang and danced for people queuing outside the working men's clubs which were popular at that time. Their "audience" would throw pennies to them. The scene was set and Vic was on her way to "treading the boards". Her dream was to play in Music Hall.

Her introduction to music hall was as a singer and a dancer. She met her first husband at this point in her life – Brian, a man who was not himself "in the business". Vic toured all over England and even did shows in America. Unfortunately, Brian contracted TB, a disease that was rampant at this time and died at a young age – despite Vic's best efforts. She nursed him through his final years.[1] Wishing to change direction, Vic met Lena Lewis and they went into partnership – "Bazaaring" – running monster raffles. Lena was the business woman and Vic took care of the "spiel". They travelled extensively even visiting places as distant as the Shetland Islands – no mean feat in those early days!! Back then, it was easier to get to America…!

At this time she met and married Peter Piper, who was a well-known musical hall artiste. He had toured with Charlie Chaplin and Stan Laurel in Fred Karno's "Mumming Birds" sketch company. Peter's speciality was marionettes but he also played piano and a variety of instruments including sleigh-bells – which were played by being mounted onto a frame where they were then struck with a couple of mallets. He also had a

---

[1] Unfortunately, there is very little biographical information available about Vic's first husband Brian who died at a young age.

"novelty aeroplane" act, which he patented, this being so unique that it is difficult to describe!

Vic met Mae Mack – who was to become a lifelong friend - in Bray, County Wicklow in 1926 whilst doing the Bazaaring, at a time when she had decided to change direction once more. She engaged a chorus line and some musicians and took them on tour to England. The dancers were scantily-clad young females, all of whom had blonde hair (a trademark of theirs). They toured England, Wales and Scotland under the name of Peter Piper's Palladiums. Peter wrote the scripts and the songs, while Vic did the choreography, production and making costumes. Meanwhile, Vic, now in her thirties, gave birth to a boy (named Brian[2] in honour of her first husband) at 29 Duke Street, Brosely in the county of Salop, England[3]. Young Brian was introduced to the stage at a very early age. However, because of the strict laws governing child performers, his parents added a couple of years to his age and said..."He is small for his age...!!" The Music Hall was like one big family and amongst her great friends in the business were Ella Shields, Little Tich, Gertie Gitana and the great Vesta Tilley. Vesta gave Vic one of her famous top hats – complete with leather hatbox – which Vic would later use in her own "male impersonation" act. She was billed as "Ireland's Vesta Tilley", wearing a beautifully tailored frock coat – trousers with a knife crease, a starched shirt, carefully polished shoes, a silver-topped cane – and *that* hat. She would enthrall the audience singing "Burlington Bertie" with all the aplomb that was unique characterisation and a voice that could "Hit off the back wall..."

---

[2] Brian's full name being Brian Walter Harold Compton (after the writer) Jackson.
[3] Salop is in Shrewsbury, England.

**The Big Hat Brigade: Grandmother Vic and adopted daughter Dot –
early 1930s**

The young Brian now began to learn the tricks of the trade. His father
taught him a variety of musical instruments and from his mother he learnt
the arts of dancing and acting. Through other performers, he was coached
in conjuring – juggling and acrobatics. Vic had previously broken her leg
during a particularly bad strenuous dance routine where she landed badly.
From then on she stuck to *choreographing* the more acrobatic dance
routines!

In the 1930s Vic and Peter decided it was time to come back to Ireland;
with a bigger, costumed show and that is exactly what they did – with the
very first chorus line in Ireland. Like so many artistes, the idea of
untapped audiences appealed to them, and like so many artistes they
joined forces with another company – Harry Lynoton. For the summer
season, Vic needed a large tent - or *booth* as it is known in the business.
The tent had to be large enough to accommodate her productions including
what was the first "chorus line" seen in Ireland, a small orchestra, and
various variety acts. As Harry had been running the Hippodrome Circus,
his tent was a good choice. Although this was "strait-laced" Ireland Vic
and Peter were unconcerned about what the clergy thought of the
"scantily-clad" dancers. Vic Loving's *Flash Parade* was a good show and
they knew it! What's more, the audiences knew it too!! It appears that

Peter Piper went back "over the water" as a programme for the "Empress Playhouse" shows in Glasgow – "Kay and his aeroplane" – the date was the eleventh of March, 1935. There must have been a lot of travelling back and forth with Peter doing his shows in Britain, and Vic running Flash Parade in Ireland.

As in England, show people in Ireland were like family – a big family which included the Circus folk. As a youngster of 13 years or age or so, the young Brian followed in the "family tradition" by occasionally performing a horse riding act with Duffy's Circus. He would do matinees afterwards performing in Vic's variety show at night. This made him a very proficient horseman, so much so that he went to train as a jockey in Cloyne, County Cork…..but the very early mornings didn't suit!!

Frank Macari, Chic and Vic Loving Comic Sketch - 1938

During the war years Brian recalled being "somewhere up North" when the air-raid sirens went off and every light went out – as they were playing in the booth when the sirens sounded they would have made a pretty easy target. There is no mention if the show went on after the "all clear" but it is presumed that it did as entertainment was scarce during that awful time….

Another bizarre consequence of the war was the lack of leg make-up!! Never mind the rationing of sugar – tea and other foodstuffs...but for the ladies of the chorus line...a short supply of leg make-up was next door to traumatic!!

This was before tights...and as stockings were also hard to come by, this was an issue of considerable importance to the leggy lovelies...!! Also for many years, the only two places to buy greasepaint were Dublin and Godwins of Kilkenny, since nowhere else stocked it.

On a sadder note, Vic's adopted daughter Dot was killed in the London Blitz, she having joined the WRVS – Women's Royal Voluntary Service.[4]

Vic had a very flamboyant nature, both in dress and demeanor. She loved fur coats, rich colours in her clothes; diamond jewellery and pearls were the norm for her!! Of course, her flamboyance also extended to her living accommodation. She had two wagons (caravans). One was for "living" in, whilst the other known as the "White Caravan" was used for entertaining guests. It got its name because everything in it was white; carpets, curtains, upholstery and even the tea service!! This is the caravan she would bring her visitors; no doubt to swap stories about others in the business, and the trials and tribulations of touring in Ireland...

Vic also had two little dogs which she treated like children! – Twinky and Judy. One was a toy terrier, the other a Yorkie, both of whom accompanied their mistress everywhere!! They would wear bows in their hair to match whatever Vic was wearing that particular day.
Fortunately, the only place which they were not allowed near was the stage, as the actors were in danger of having their ankles gnawed off!!

---

[4] The WRVS (formerly the Women's Royal Voluntary Service, known until 1956 as the Women's Voluntary Service) is a voluntary organisation whose remit is to help people who are in need throughout Britain. It was initially titled the WVS and founded in 1938 by Stella Isaacs, the Marchioness of Reading. Its initial function was as a British women's organisation which aimed to aid civilians during war-time. As a voluntary organisation, the WVS did not have a compulsory uniform and many WVS members who may not have been able to afford the uniform went about their work wearing a simple WVS badge on their lapels. The work of the WVS covered a very broad spectrum but one of its primary duties involved the organisation of first aid courses in the cities that were thought to be likely targets for German army bombers missions during World War II.

This would certainly have disrupted the whole proceedings, and the only person allowed to do that was her son Brian!

Vic was one of those eccentric showbiz characters! – to say the least…and she needed to be…!! Being superstitious helped her eccentricity. No whistling in the dressing room…No washing costumes…No real flowers on stage…No cleaning the drumkit before the show…!! She didn't like the colour green although many of the original costumes were of varying shades of green. These were the costumes and props she bought for auctions at the "big houses" all over Ireland. She had a huge stock of frocks – uniforms, shoes, hats – as well as the costumes she made for the dance routines.

Through years of travelling around Ireland Vic had her fair share of altercations with local clergy. In Cappamore, County Limerick, she was denounced from the pulpit with the words – "that show should be called Flesh Parade – with the amount of skin on show". The priest then went on to tell the good people of the parish not to go to the show. They responded to this by packing the hall each night thereafter…!!

Another time in Mill Street, County Cork, the priest boarded up the door of the hall. After getting one of the men to remove the boards and let the audience in, Vic followed the priest up the street and told him in no uncertain terms what she thought of his way of doing business! She had to stand her ground on many occasions. When you take into consideration that Vic was a woman who ran her own company in the Ireland of those years – it was *not* an easy task!!

There was another particular occasion when she would not let someone get the better of her. The show was preparing to leave and the local policeman decided to be very officious - without result! The company was taking down the booth and the Guard approached Vic in connection with an "untaxed vehicle". This car had recently been shipped over from England by Vic, and was being towed, rather than being driven, as Dublin was the place where cars were taxed. The Guard would hear no explanation and told her that the car was staying put…and that was that". Vic then called over two of the tilt (tent) men and told them to break up the car with the words. "If I'm not having it – neither are you…" She departed that village and never appeared with her show there again...!!

Vic Loving and son Chic in 1927

Brian Piper – (Chic) doing his Horse Act which appeared in Duffys Circus – early 1930s

Up to then, Brian had been using the name "the Chicago Kid" for his performances. His father had died on Saint Patrick's Day, 1942, when Brian was sixteen and was buried in Lismore, County Waterford. Vic had many friends there including Lady Cavendish otherwise known as Adele Astaire – sister of the world-renowned Fred. It was she who christened the young Brian – "the Pocket Fred Astaire" –as he did a "top hat and tails act" which emulated the fabulous Fred…

Peter Piper's gravestone bears an inscription of musical notes and the words "just a song at twilight". Brian now took his father's stage name – Piper.

In time, Vic decided to have a tent specially designed to mirror a real theatre. This was custom-built in a rectangular shape rather than the usual circular style. A lorry which held chairs, props and costumes by day, was magically transformed by night, when it became a draught-free sound proof dressing room. Having her own tent gave Vic the freedom to get a tóber (field) anywhere for her shows It would have been used only the summer months, since, for obvious practical reasons the halls were always used during the winter. And many of these halls were not luxurious by any means – but that's another story!!

Below – "Matinee-Idol"Chic Playing His Guitar – 1950s

Vic Loving's Round Tent which she had while working with Harry Lynton in the 1930s

Vic with one of her Caravans complete with Canopy – 1950s

Tilt-men erecting the Booth

Brian was now becoming the lynchpin of the show and once again he changed his name; the time to the name that everyone would remember him by – Chic Kay!! Following in the footsteps of other great comics associated with *Flash Parade* – he was to become *the* comedian of the company, taking over from Dan Mooney. As the "write ups" from this era show, Chic was popular with both young and old alike, being one of the group of comics who did not do "blue gags". He went on to become one of Ireland's best-known comedians, and like a lot of showmen he was multi-talented. Of course, Chic was like so many of the eligible – and not so eligible – young men who were in the business, the girls fancied him like mad. Even the dancers in the company were smitten, but Vic had her girls chaperoned – "no dalliances allowed"!! One of the conversations I had with a "fan" of the show who used to live in Bruree, County Limerick described how her friend used to practically camp outside Chic's wagon in the hope of getting a glimpse of her "idol"…young innocent days…!!

Chic was a real practical joker. Having a photographic memory, he knew the lines of the plays before anyone did, so that gave him plenty of time to play pranks during rehearsals. When this became too much for the rest of the cast…mayhem ensued…and they *"corpsed"* (dried up). That was Vic's cue to "fire" the whole company!! That was pretty much the norm…Chic messing and Vic declaring "the show is closed" and making a dramatic stage night – It was then left to Frank Macari to talk her around and to finish rehearsal. Chic took every opportunity to wind everyone up…and Vic always took the bait!!

Chic also loved "gadgets" and the latest in "special effects" fascinated him. One story relates to when he was using "squibs" – small explosive devices – in a production of "The Informer". There were people from another company in the audience that night and they were really taken with this effect – so much so that they asked Chic for a couple of these squibs. He handed them over - with strict instructions to put them into a safe receptacle! Some time later, when that company set off the devices during a dramatic scene – the audience found themselves covered in a blanket of fine white dust and chippings…The "safe" receptacle had turned out to be a "toilet" at the side of the stage…!!

Another story concerns the "summer season" which was so good it went into the autumn…The show was still in the booth, and each evening it got progressively colder. Vic decided to put on a "Hawaiian" scene; all the dancers dressed in grass skirts with flowered leis (Hawaiian garlands) but shivering and turning blue with frozen smiles! As they were doing a "hula", on walked Chic togged out in an oversized coat, scarf, hat, boots and gloves. At this juncture not only did the dancers collapse into helpless laughter, but so did the audience – who thought it part of the act! Even Vic could not suppress a smile whilst, at the same time, admonishing Chic for "acting the sod"!!

Another "dancers" story concerns two girls who joined *Flash Parade* and were supposed to be expert in the art of dance. They were being choreographed in some of the steps for a particularly intricate piece when they declared that "they knew it all"…!! On went the show to the dismay of Vic, but also the chorus line who went the wrong way in the middle of a twirl! The entire line were knocked flat on their bums, to the laughter and thunderous applause of the audience…Vic was *not* amused!!

Chic was a "handsome devil" as the photos show. He had an easy charm got on with both men and women alike. He was very much the "devil-may-care, footloose-and-fancy-free kind of character. Cosseted all his life, private tutor for schooling and private tutors for his schooling. Although it does appear he occasionally attended *some* schools, as the school attendance act form - (from Ramelton, County Donegal, dated 1938, when Chic was aged twelve, will testify) - the bulk of his learning came from "the school of life"...

He was the apple of his mother's eye and she doted on him. He could do no wrong...and any woman did lay claim to him would have her hands full...!! Eventually someone *did* take Chic on...

Nancy Hoey grew up in and around Dublin city. From an early age she developed a love of the theatre from her father John, who often brought her to performances at the Queen's Theatre. She attended dancing school, and along with her best friend Peggy Keogh, she performed regularly – singing and dancing their way through many of the school's productions – the bug had bitten!! So much so that the teenage Nancy went off to Gerry Broadbin's Happydrome Parade in 1944...in Ennis, County Clare. In her own words – "Newmarket, County Cork". I'd heard of the Chicago Kid and Vic Loving and their terrific show. The girls, the glamour, the costumes, lights and scenery, trucks and cars, (Gerry Broadbin's company travelled by train!) and the luxurious caravans...Everybody but everybody was suitably impressed...! Reg Dale, a musician, on Broadbin's Show brought herself and some of the cast to see Peter Piper's grave in Lismore, County Waterford. She didn't "realize it then but she would marry the son of this man and become the daughter of the famous Vic Loving".

My first sighting of the Chicago Kid was when he strolled into the hall, dressed in a burberry mac, a well-cut suit and two-tone shoes. His hat tilted to the back of his head. To me, he was straight out of Hollywood. In retrospect, he was like a character out of a movie. Later, I discovered he was a dynamic performer. I'd not seen someone so talented, but he seemed so unaware of it. To him, it was all simply a job, the family business, a bit of a chore to him. He really wanted to be a jockey..."

Nancy Hoey joined Vic Loving's company as a singer and dancer, but Vic had other ideas. Thrown in at the deep end, Nancy's first appearance in a play was that of an elderly woman. Her next part was Katie Fox in the "The Informer". Nancy was just sixteen years old at the time...In the touring shows everyone was expected to be an all-rounder – and most were!!

Peggy Keogh then joined the show. She and Nancy both loved the travelling. The glamour of life "on the road"! Getting their own digs (accommodation)! The boys! Vic's policy of "chaperoning" as undertaken by the older girls, meant that no chances were taken on the courting front! When you consider that some of the female performers, some of them still quite young – had travelled over from England to join the show – then Vic had to be careful…

One of the young girls who joined Vic's show was Mary Rowe from Bruff, County Limerick. She had an amazing voice which she'd used as a youngster to entertain the other children in Bruff. She would change costumes and put on a show starring…herself! She loved showbusiness so much she got herself onto Flash Parade. Vic knew talent when she saw it and Mary could do wicked impersonations of Vic herself – performing her "male act". Mary has put what she has learned in her days of touring to great effect and has gone onto act on many an illustrious stage – winning awards in drama festivals and appearing on television and in a variety of film roles.

Chic and Nancy Hoey started to "date" but as often as not they would be (chaperoned) accompanied on these dates by the cast of the show. Around Christmas-time Chic worked in the *Capitol* in Princes Street.

In Nancy's own words – "…During his holidays from (his mother's) Vic Loving's show. Miss Loving, Peggy Keogh, Fred Macari, Billy Seymour and I all want to see the show. Seán Mooney, Mick Eustace were in the cast of this Christmas show along with the dancers known as the Capitol Girls. Everyone enjoyed the show but Vic was furious as Brian had worn ….red socks!"

One story told by the late Sonny Coll – from Bruree – describes a group of the performers heading off to the cinema in Kilmallock, County Limerick. Just as they were about to enter the cinema, Vic and her manager Frank Macari came tearing up the street in a car, the tyres screeching. On being ordered to – "get back to the show" – the group climbed back into the Chic's car, fairly miffed at having missed the film! Vic's rules had to be adhered to and that was the beginning and the end of it. And there was definitely "no going out with men" – not even if that man happened to be Vic's own son...! The rules were applied in the same way to everybody in that touring company, irrespective of who they were…Eventually, Chic and Nancy did get married – and had two children, both of whom also went into the business (weekends only), thereby following in the footsteps of their parents, grandparents and the generations before them again.

Nancy and Chic – Musical Double-Act – 1950s

Nancy Hoey performing Ballet – c. 1950s

Vivienne Victoria (moi) and my brother "wee Kenneth" as he was affectionately known) did parts in plays and duplicated our folks "double act", singing harmonies to guitar accompaniment.

Not only was Frank Macari Vic's manager, but they also lived together (years before it became fashionable to do so). He, too, was highly talented and became Chic's "straight man" in comedy routines and sketches. He also played roles in a number of the plays. He is best remembered in his role as a distinctly nasty "piece of work" playing a Black and Tan[5] in "The Informer". He was even hissed at in the street in one village! He was best known for his wizardry on the "electric piano accordion" and was the first to bring that instrument into the country. Frank was also our godfather, and him being an Italian was the source of much mirth…

Vic Loving brought colour and gaiety to the Irish Travelling shows with a cornucopia of costumed revues, pantos, scenas, variety and drama. She was always trying out new ideas including special effects such as "black lighting" (ultraviolet). As the first show in Ireland to do so, she put this new technique to good use in a dance routine called the "dancing skeletons", which mesmerized audiences in many counties. She insisted on authenticity for all of her productions, having gleaned props and costumes – some of which survive today – from the "Big House"[6] auctions throughout the country. It is reported that Vic toured with a total stock of two thousand costumes, costumes whose style ranged from the Victorian period to the 1950s. This included the chorus line costumes she designed and made herself. Vic was known as the "Sequin Queen" because of the sparkle and shimmer they presented to countless audiences. Having so many changes of costume meant she could make a whole show look completely different every night from variety right through to drama. Hers was one of the only travelling shows that supplied costumes to all of its players. In my collection, I have costumes which bear the names of the various girls inked into the bodices. These costumes were handed on to each girl who replaced a previous dancer…Vic 's show was the last

---

[5] A member of a paramilitary force recruited in Britain and sent to Ireland as part of the Royal Irish Constabulary to suppress the Sinn Fein rebellion of 1919 to 1921. Although it was established to target the Irish Republican Army, it became notorious through its numerous attacks on the Irish civilian population. Together with the Auxiliary Division of the RIC (the 'Auxies'), they acquired a reputation for ferocity and indiscipline.
[6] The "Big House" is a euphemism for the large houses situated on landed estates that are/were owned by the Anglo-Irish gentry.

company to play Hartigan's Hall in Castleconnell, County Limerick – a fact which she was very proud of.

Vic and her Dancing Girls in a Scene from "Marble Arch"

Vic finally closed the show in Croom, County Limerick, where she had parked her wagon and one of her trucks – in Halpin's Field. She and Frank Macari stayed there until they moved to Drogheda, County Louth. They both continued to entertain, doing "spots" at various venues, cabarets, and shows. They then moved to Shankill, County Dublin. Frank, not being married to Vic went to London one weekend and got hitched...to a woman he had met at Ballroom Dancing classes. Vic ended her days in the Jewish Nursing Home in Dublin but not before quoting in a newpaper article – "Old troopers don't die, they just fade away".

Vic died in 1974 and is buried in the Jewish Cemetery in Dolphin's Barn, Dublin. Chic died in 1987 and is buried in Shanganagh Cemetery, Shankill, County Dublin. Nancy died in 2007 and is buried beside Chic. Their gravestone designed by me represents all the facets of their combined talents...Chic's guitar – Nancy's tap shoes – Comedy and theatrical masks engraved on black marble. As we don't do "big" funerals in our family – I wanted to mark their passing with something a little unusual for their headstone…!!

FLASH PARADE: PLAYLIST

List of the Plays Performed by Vic Loving's *Flash Parade*

The McCormack Brothers[1]
The Wayfarer
Gerry the Tramp
Gaslight
White Sister
Uncle Tom's Cabin
Peg o' my Heart
Sweeney Todd
Road by the River[2]
Charlie's Aunt
Ten Commandments
Alice Ben Bolt
The Informer
Shadow of a Gunman
Children of Fatima
Going My Way
Face at the Window
Three Weeks
Night Must Fall
Mr. Pimple's Plunge
Roseanna
Rebel's Wife/The Wearing of the Green
Little Nellie Kelly
Annie Laurie
Hungarian Horror[3]

---

[1] This play was written by William Seymour. William Seymour was a member of the "Fit-ups" who had been a journalist at one time. He used his skills at shorthand to "jot" down the story when he went to the cinema. He then went back to the show and the cast worked on a edited version of the orginal.

[2] This play was written by Frank O'Donovan, later known as "Batty Brennan" in the Riordans. Frank had previously toured with his own show.

[3] This play was written by William Seymour.

Song of Bernadette
Ben Macree or Mona
Murder in the Red Barn/Maria Marten
Lady Audley's Secret
Ladies in Retirement/Crime in the Marshes
Smilin' Through[4]
East Lynne
Royal Divorce/Napoleon and Josephine
Midnight Wedding
Sonny Boy
Woman in Red
Mugs for Each[5]
Magan
The Secret Tattoo[6]
Noreen Bawn
Matinee
Davy Crockett
Danny Boy
Cisco Kid
Pantos
Babes in the Wood
Cinderella
Dick Whittington
Sinbad the Sailor

---

[4] Vic played the part of Sir John in this play.
[5] This play was written by William Seymour.
[6] This play was written by V.Loving.

Some Revues Performed by by Vic Loving's Flash Parade

[These revues were performed in a style that was a combination of music hall and spectacular musical comedy]

Tragedy of a Clown[7]
Story of Pagliagi
Legion of the Lost
Russian[8]
Siberian[9]
Round the World in Two Hours[10]
Old English
Red Sails in the Sunset
Radio Revels Revue
Down in Dixie
Push Off/Head of Nero
Rose of Tralee
Li Ching

A Scena Performed by Vic Loving's Flash Parade

Dangerous Dan McGrew
White Christmas
Alice Blue Gown

Pantos Performed by Vic Loving's Flash Parade

Dick Whittington
Babes in the Wood
Sinbad the Sailor
Cinderella

---

[7] This revue was written by Peter Piper.
[8] This revue was written by Peter Piper.
[9] This revue was written by Peter Piper.
[10] This revue was written by Peter Piper.

SHOWBIZ KIDS: GROWING ON THE ROAD

Nancy with Vikki and Ken

Before I start it should be pointed out that my sense of humour borders on the caustic as those who know me can testify to…I was born in Father Matthew Terrace, Clonmel, County Tipperary, in the home of Jack Delahunty (brother of well-known band leader Mick). My parents were good friends of the Delahuntys and Jack's wife Chris had suggested that my mother should give birth to me at their house – because of previous complications and the fact that they had a brilliant doctor. So, on April the fourth, 1954 I arrived into the world!! As we only stayed in Clonmel for two weeks I did not get a good look at the place…that came later! At two and a half weeks, I first "appeared" on stage in Pallasgreen, County Limerick carried on by a very proud grandmother Vic. I promptly fell asleep – so my memories of this moment are hazy!!

The next time I trod the boards was in Moneenroe, County Kilkenny, when I was 3! All through the summer months, Eve Betesh, one of the company, tried to persuade me to go on during a matinee. Every Sunday she would dress me in one of my best frocks – much to my parents amusement. However, given that I would regularly act the prima donna on a Sunday – I refused!

Then, on one particularly cold Sunday afternoon, I toddled on stage wrapped up to within an inch of my life – and sang *Tammy...* – a popular song in the Fifties as recoded by Debbie Reynolds – (I still have the sheet music somewhere). Dressed in a winter coat, boats and a furry hat – which I hated! – I was accompanied by my dad Chic Kay on guitar. When I finished, our manager Frank Macari, strode up through the centre aisle and presented me with a 10 shilling note, which Chic promptly tried to pocket! The audience, who were mainly children, booed him until I got my money back…!

We loved the traveling but hated having to go to school: the thoughts of starting in another place each week or two, trying to make new friends and cope with new sets of lessons was horrendous! My very first memory of school is of being handed a slate and a piece of chalk. I thought it very odd – given that, by the age of six, I could read and had been using pencil and paper for quite some time – as I loved to draw. Ken and myself never did learn to speak the Irish language as we both had very "posh" accents, the bulk of the company having come from England originally. Because of this we were totally ignored – or barely tolerated! – in some schools. Going from memory, the best schools we attended were Protestant as I could get to wear my trousers – being very much the tomboy – this suited me very well!! Now I understand why it was that so many parents sent their kids to boarding schools. We moved around so much that our names must are probably on every old school roll book in Ireland…!

As "show kids", we were always set apart from the local children we met whilst touring around – by the very fact that we appeared on stage, acting out parts which transported us to worlds which only other people could dream of…

Being "different" had its "cringe-making" moments too, however. Like the time the local parish priest presented us with a box of chocolates at the end of a show. He told the assembled audience – (which included our classmates) that he had never met such "…cultured, well-mannered and beautifully-spoken children and that the children of the parish would do well to take note…"!

We still had several days to go in that school in Castlecomer, County Kilkenny!!

As the eldest of two, I felt it was my job to look out for my "little brother". Once in Croom, County Limerick a little yob threatened Ken with a penknife. He hadn't allowed for Ken's "minder" though and I proceeded to wallop this young fella – both he and his penknife ended up in a mud-filled ditch!! When I went back and told my parents what had happened I got a clout – not for fighting, but for breaking a brand new thermos flask I had received as a present from some relatives in California. As a footnote to this story, we all went into Limerick city to replace the thermos and because were the thousandth customer in the shop – we got it for free! Delighted at getting "something for nothing", we returned home to find that it leaked!!

The school in Croom had been an old Church and most of the windows were missing glass. The main room was divided by a partition into six classes, three on each side. Rather confusing when each class was doing different lessons! The only heat in the room came from two fireplaces which the teachers had next to their desks. It's a wonder anyone got an education – between the racket going on in the room and trying not to freeze to death!!

Something else that made me stand out in different schools was my uniform. I had been bought a "stunning" green creation – a pinafore with pleats. If anything was ever designed to make me look like a dork, then this was it!! As luck would have it, me and my yucky green gymslip attended all the convent schools where they wore *blue* uniforms. So I looked like a lone Christmas tree in the middle of the deep blue sea – talk about blending in…!!

On occasions we were made to practically feel invisible, and I remember one, and I still remember one incident very well. Ken and I were sitting at the back of the class (out of sight?!). The nun's "pet" was up at a desk in the front of the class. The reason for this soon became apparent – this child, golden-haired, blue-eyed with the face of angel – but *not* the voice – I hasten to add – was made to entertain anyone of any "importance" with her rendition of "Scarlet Ribbons"! This rendition of the song was always truly awful! She sang in a high, scratchy off-key voice, with the benevolent nun standing beside her enraptured with this "talent". To the duo from the Flash Parade, it was *not* music to our ears! I often wonder if the rest of the class had to endure this torture, forever, and how come we were never asked to sing? To this day, I cannot listen to "Scarlet Ribbons"…!!

My brother Ken was obviously more wonderful than me as he first appeared on stage playing drums…at two and a half!! Well…he did have Chic as a father…! One day whilst driving to the next date, Ken and I were sitting in the back seat of the car when we began to sing together in harmony. Having a good ear for music…and he still has…Ken picked up harmonising from my dad. Chic formed a "double act" with my mother. Dad handed Ken a ukulele which he said was a "miniature guitar for a small boy". I am sure there were many in the audience who could not get over this small child's dexterity on the guitar, especially when Dad was "doing all the work" in the wings!! The first place we performed our double-act in was Skerries in County Dublin. One of the posters in my collection has Ken billed as the "Miniature Tommy Steele"…and myself as the "Pocket Soubrette"…!![17]

The things that parents (and grandmothers) do to their children!!

Of course, following in the footsteps of many showbiz kids, I went on to play the part of "Little Willie" in that good old melodrama "East Lynne". When I got too ancient – aged eight and lanky – Ken took over…anyway – he was better-looking than me!! I got the opportunity to play another role in that play – the part of Suzanne the French maid. I really enjoyed all the make-up and "padding" that was designed to turn me into a teenager. Best of all was being able to give "guff" to my dad who played the dastardly villain – Sir Francis Levison.

> Him: "To the devil with you Suzanne"
> Me: "After you Monsieur"

I also had parts in other plays - pantos – matinees – and scenas – All that glitz and glamour!!! These are some of the productions that stand out vividly for me in my childhood memory. The revue "Around the World in

---

[17] The phrase "pocket soubrette" originates in the French language and it means "little maiden". This was often a minor female role as a pert flirtatious lady's maid in a comedy.

Eighty Minutes" was written by my grandfather Peter Piper – a revue in which Granny Vic played a Chinese Mandarin complete with exotic costumes, coal-rimmed eyes…and a very long moustache. The whole company dressed in an array of equally fabulous costumes from "all over the world". The pantos were always fantastic. Ken and I played the kids in "Babes in the Woods". I remember being a fairy queen in one, my wand and crown having been made by Frank Macari, the surfaces covered in iris (glass-glitter). I really loved that outfit and the costumes for that panto were amazing – all satins, velvets, chiffons and taffetas. There were coats and cloaks – wonderful wigs and hats! Beautiful scenery which depicted countryside and castles. Granny Vic performed as Principal Boy and dressed in breathtaking outfits covered with pearls, sequins and diamante. Chic played one of the ugly sisters with Frank Macari playing the other. One of the funniest sketches on stage was Chic as the ugly sister "getting ready for the ball" behind a scrim-cloth in silhouette. He had the whole audience in hysterics as he donned his "underwear and stockings" in his own inimitable fashion- a little "risqué" but never crude…

I would often sit for hours watching Chic create different characters through the magic that is make-up. He made his own masks, scars and wigs. He could alter his young handsome face into a gruesome fiend. My mother was so enamoured with his transformations that she sent a photo of Chic as "Sweeney Todd" to her parents and telling them – "This is the man I'm going out with". To which her father's response was – "That ould fella…?!!"

I watched my grandmother making sets of costumes on her Singer showing machine. She bought fabric by the bale and sequins by the yard. Her attention to detail was fabulous. The transformation of fabric into a fairytale Cinderella costume or a Japanese kimono: it made me follow in her footsteps.

It is said that you learn from experience and if this is true – then I learnt from the best…

Chic Kay in cowboy pose beside one of Vic Loving's trucks

All of that observation would pay off in later life…memories of standing in one of the big lorries which housed our huge collection of costumes - watching my mother Nancy organising sets of dancing outfits and gowns needed for that night's performance. She was in charge of wardrobe for many years and knew where every shoe, hat, bag and prop was packed. She needed to know – seeing as Vic Loving travelled a very large number of costumes – all of which were changed periodically, so that the show always looked fresh. Vic owned a small cottage in Bruree, County Limerick, which she also used as a store for these costumes. Every few months, all the scenery, props and costumes were exchanged for another batch – thereby giving a whole new look and texture to the productions. My earliest memories of the village of Bruree are the smell of fresh bread from the local bakery, and Annie Coll giving me lemonade and biscuits. We were staying with the Coll family at the time because the axle on our caravan had snapped – and was being repaired. Annie's offerings were quite a treat as my mother was quite strict about us "eating rubbish" and "ruining our teeth". Annie bore a striking resemblance to my grandmother and were often mistaken for each other. Sonny Coll joined our show in Bruree, by telling my gran he was an expert dancer and musician – The piano he could play and he was a real raconteur but as regards dancing – not a chance! Vic was choreographing a new dance routine and she asked Sonny if he would support the females who were doing a pyramid formation…he couldn't and they all ended up in a heap on the floor!! What he was good at was spoofing…which is why himself and Chic were always up to something nefarious – such as annoying the hell out of my grandmother!

Other incidents spring to mind – such as the time in Piltown, County Kilkenny, just before the evening show, when Dad asked me to fetch his suit from the dressing room of the hall, which had once been an old church. The evening light that slanted through the old windows cast eerie shadows over walls and chairs, dark corners took on spooky shapes…
Increasing my footsteps, which echoed ominously on the wooden flooring, I finally made it to the door. Half-afraid of what might be lurking there on the other side, I stood for several minutes, trying to build up the courage to open it…

When I eventually did, I nearly fainted…hanging on the wall was one of my dad's horror masks and a costume to match…!! I grabbed the suit and ran like hell…!

Funnily enough - during the daylight hours, I spent all of my time drawing in the hallway, on a huge blackboard with coloured chalks. As they say, lighting *does* set the mood…!

It was in Athlone, County Westmeath that I got a crystal necklace from a young and ardent fan, who wanted me to be his girlfriend. I remember at the time feeling rather disappointment because I would have preferred a bag of sweets. Well…what would one expect from a six year old?

As kids we only remember the summers as being hot and sunny. For touring with the booth, good weather was a bonus. One time, however, that was not the case. In Quin, County Clare, a storm blew up all of a sudden and got worse as the day went on. The booth was taken down and we all went indoors but our small wagon started to rock. My mother got so freaked out that we moved into Granny Vic's higher and heavier wagon. Luckily the storm blew itself out before any serious damage could be done.

When I was seven, I made my Holy Communion in Kilavullen, County Cork. I went to the local school there and the preparations for the big day were not a happy experience for me. My mother asked the teacher there to improve my arithmetic, something which is *still* not one of my strong points. The said teacher proceeded to humiliate me in front of the entire class by trying to send me to "low babies" (junior infants) whereupon I retaliated by throwing my schoolbag at a glass door. It didn't break, and, and after much grovelling on my mother's part, I was asked to come back into the class and "allowed" to go through the whole "charade" – for, to me, at that age, a charade or a performance of sorts – this is what all of this was - the dressing up in a fancy frock and the learning of various lines off-by-heart – Didn't I do *that* on the stage! The only difference this time was that I stood out from the rest – literally!! – Wearing a big stiff American slip under my frock, I looked like a big Christmas cake. That was the only time I remember Dad going to church – as I reminded him going up the street – whereupon I was quickly told in hushed tones "Nantee" (No). The only time he was religious was when he played a priest in the play *Going my Way*!

To add insult to injury, our lovely field spaniel Brutus died that day – and, to cap it all – I spent the spent the rest of the day in someone's back garden in Cork, being told "not to dirty my dress"!! I did get to use *that* dress again in one of my Gran's scenas – *White Christmas*. This involved choreographing some local children – all girls – to walk around the stage in time to that well-loved song of the same name. On the day of the performance, I would help to tear up used white tickets – to make snowflakes which were thrown from the "flies". The beautiful glittering scenery made it a magical experience both for the girls on stage, and - of course – their friends and relatives who came to see them make their debuts...

Some ladies who lived in Kilfinane, County Limerick used come to see my large collection of costumes as relating to the "fit-up" days and told me of their childhood joy at being amongst the "White Christmas children" of those selfsame days.

One of the times that I remember being affected and really upset at a performance was in Glenworth, County Cork. After Ken and I had finished our "spot" in the variety section of the show, we were allowed to stay up and watch that night's play – *The Informer* – my dad playing the role of Gypo Nolan. When it came to that point in the play where Gypo gets shot, my Dad dragged himself on stage, pouring (fake) blood and moaning. At this point Ken and I began to weep, wondering "what's happened to our Daddy?" - and getting more and more hysterical by the minute. Eventually, a member of the cast named Mary McMahon had to drag us out…no more late nights for us after that for a while…! Seeing our Dad perform his Elvis Presley impersonation (the earlier model) on stage provided some lighter moments. He would strike the pose. With hair hanging over one eye, guitar slung low, and the "look" – the girls in the audience would rush to the front of the stage screaming and swooning. My only thought was: - "Why are they screaming and shouting at my Daddy?" As Vic Loving's grandchildren, we were often invited out to meals with our parents and our grandmother, usually by the "gentry". I don't recall being mightily impressed by the big houses and swanky table settings – although, if it was "high tea", we might get to cream crackers and jam tarts. As small beings usually we were always "starving"…our real bugbear concerning food were the *cheese* sandwiches, we got *every* day going to school. We often swapped our "healthy" food *jam* sandwiches…Now that was a real treat…!

One of the gentry I speak of was Lady Doneraile. Our family was one of the few who were granted permission to park our wagons on her estate in Doneraile, County Cork. She used to give us tours of her beautiful house, her lovely fruit and vegetable garden. On the lake next to her house there were swans, and we had donkey rides – it was quite magical. I always enjoyed the company of this genteel lady who made plenty of time for these two young children…

Another titled person who enjoyed our show was Sir Harold Barry[18], who resided at "The Grange", a beautiful house in Castleconnell, County Limerick. Sir Harold became great friends with my father and mother, so much so that my mother celebrated her twenty-first birthday at "the

---

[18] Sir Harold Barry was only one amongst many of the "gentry" who frequented the shows. Nancy Hoey – "English couple who used to stay in the Greystones Hotel, Wicklow - who came to see the show each night – later wrote to me as "the girl on the Irish pound"…Later I learned that she was Lady Hazel Lavery, the wife of the famous painter."

Grange". That was before Ken and I arrived on the scene. My parents would go to Limerick in Sir Harold's chauffeur-driven car which he would lend to Chic to go "shopping" in Limerick. As Chic normally drove on MG, this was really doing it in style! It was in this MG, too, that he tried to teach my mother to drive, Nancy thought she was doing really well until the day she nearly ran my Granny Vic down...I think there may have been a little "coolness" there for a while after that...! Vic Loving's company was the last show to play Hartigan's Hall in Castleconnell and of all her productions – *Song of Bernadette* – is remembered with particular affection.

My mother had decreed that we were not to be spoiled by being given sweets or chocolates – but we always thwarted her plans by going to Granny Vic who had a plentiful supply of goodies. Once, we were parked beside a sweet factory and we had been given some money – so we went to the back door where one could obtain a bucket-load of broken sugary sweets for a couple of pence – which we duly did! Ken, being ever tactful, didn't stuff his face, whereas I did while sitting in a quiet corner – until, feeling decidedly queasy – I was put to bed. It was a few days before my mother found out, when she discovered Ken's stash of goodies hidden under the mattress!

Since friends of our parents often came to the show, they didn't need to pay for tickets – so they would "bring something for the kids..."

In Bray, County Wicklow this happened to be the biggest bag of jelly beans we'd ever seen...! As we were "put to bed" for the night, the lure of the goodies was just too much. As the evening was warm, the windows were left open in the wagon. The same can't be said for our bedroom door as it was locked...So, with this in mind, I put the ladder from the bunk-beds out the window - climbed out – put it against the *other* window where the jellybeans were – climbed in that window – took then and...then back to the bedroom. We munched our way through three-quarters of the bag, afterwards returning the rest of the bag to where I had taken it from. The next morning mother's face was a picture as she tried to figure out how the bag of sweets had shrunk overnight! We never did tell her, but given that our only treat was a small bar of chocolate every Friday – any form of "illegal booty" was always welcome!! Parties were a regular feature of show-life – for the adults that is – not for us children. There was always a party going on somewhere after each show. World-famous tenor Joseph Locke's house in Ballybunion, County Kerry, was a regular haunt for a "knees-up" I remember the Ballybunion of long ago with great affection because of the many days we spent on the beach playing with my friends Janie, Carrie and Kim of the Williams family who owned the cinema and the amusements there. Apart from the fact that I nearly drowned there twice – didn't put me off the place – there was one day where Janie, Carrie, Kim, Ken and I decided that we wanted to make a few bob for ourselves by staging a matinee. We had practiced our wonderful singing, choreography, and just about everything else – all morning. Ken was sent out to do the *spiel* at the gate to the *tóber* (field) where the booth and the wagons were parked…so far so good…!

A "large audience", consisting of our mother and Eileen (Williams) – i.e. their mother – were in attendance. All was going well, as we each went through our various "acts". This was until sniggering turned to loud guffaws at my attempts at tap-dancing! Whereupon, showing my true professionalism, I promptly began whingeing and rushed from the stage - into the wings. Then Ken's turn came and – and he was well into his drum solo…a loud voice boomed out. "Shut that bloody racket up!!" My grandmother had been woken from her afternoon nap and was somewhat disgruntled as a result…no wonder she never needed a mike!! By now, tears of mirth were running down the faces of those in the "audience". To add insult to injury –and after much sulking – we had to give them back their "ticket" money (6d in old money). That was our first and last attempt at running our own show!!

Having said this there was one day in Ballybunion when two old dears came to book a couple of seats for the show. Mae Mack watched as they approached our caravan, and spotting someone through the window, the women started to shout through the glass. When they got no response, they became more and more agitated and impatient and eventually gave up – walking away while muttering about "people being deaf". What they didn't know was that they had actually been speaking to Caesar, our Great golden Labrador, who thought all of this attention was terrific fun!!

Caesar really enjoyed Ballybunion too as he was forever sneaking up behind unsuspecting tots and slurping their ice creams and lollies. He also loved going to the local tennis court and golf course, as we discovered when moving the wagon at the end of the season…Underneath was a huge hoard of balls of *every* description! – all of which were quickly returned anonymously before we left town. He also used to follow Frank Macari to the church every Sunday. He would plonk himself up at the altar where the people going to Communion would trip over him on the way back to their seats, much to their chagrin of both the priest and the rest of the Mass-goers. Everyone knew the big dog from the show – and being a Labrador – he was as daft as a brush...and loved to chew everything in sight...One morning Dad, too tried to give Caesar his early morning run, tied him with a long lead to the towbar...Everyone promptly went back to sleep. When we finally got up and opened the door, Caeasar had chewed his way through the end of the caravan – leaving a gaping hole! After that incident, he was always given a proper run in the mornings! There was another time when that daft dog got an unexpected walk – from Ballyhale to Mullinavat – in County Kilkenny! He made friends with a passer-by – (or should that be his sandwiches!) – a man who, for whatever reason, decided Caesar was lost. He looped a belt through the dog's collar and set off. An urgent SOS went out from my grandmother – who even announced from the stage that there would be a "substantial reward of ten-shillings for the return of this valuable dog...!!" My father then received a frantic message from the police in Mullinavat to say – "Come and collect this mad animal!" Apparently, they had put Caesar into a room but every time they tried to feed him, he lunged at the door, barking furiously at the indignity of being locked up. As soon as he saw Chic, Caesar, once more became the docile mutt that we all knew and loved. Of course, we were all delighted to have him back, and he was very carefully watched after that!!

As Caesar got older, he became a brilliant watchdog. One night, having been let out for his "after-show walk", we heard a frantic barking coming from inside the hall, which like everything else in those days was unlocked. My Dad grabbed one of his "blanks" guns and fired off a shot in the direction of the rapidly disappearing figure. Next day, it was all around the village that "the shot" had narrowly missed this chap's ear, and he'd "just been curious to see what was in the hall"...not having been to that night's show. No doubt, he was in no hurry to find out after that!!

Another night in Tyrellspass, County Westmeath, Caesar once again let Dad know there was something amiss. When he went out, our trusty "security guard" had trapped a drunk in the back seat of our car, which this chap had fled to in an effort to get away from "the fearsome brute". On getting out of the car, he tried to steady himself by putting his hand on Dad's shoulder but found himself pinned to the ground by this huge dog – who only let go after being given the command. That was the last time anyone tried to take a short-cut home...!! Winning a dog show in the 1960s, Caesar was presented with a sack of spuds by Lady Carew!

"Travelling day" was a regular feature of our life, when we would leave one hall to go to another. Most of the time the "fit-up" was dismantled the night before, which involved taking apart scenery, packing trunks, stowing away chairs, lights, props etc. Early the next morning – usually on a Monday – we would travel onto the next date…I got used to seeing some grotty hall or unused church being transformed into a proper theatre: I just took it for granted…

If one was needed, the stage was slotted together, the frame which held the roll-drop scenery being erected piece by piece. The "drops" were large painted cloths of canvas, suspended between wooden rollers – which allowed different scenes to be raised or lowered as required. Frank Macari was an extremely gifted artist and along with my Dad painted some beautiful backdrops. Both sides of the roll-drops were painted thus extending the range of scenes. Sometimes two or three sets of *tabs* (curtains) would be pulled between acts. The stage was lit by huge gantry lights, reflector lamps and small spotlights which were used for the "pin-wheels". These were large circles cut out at the edges and coloured gels put in their place. These were mainly used in dance routines for added effect. Then came some of the instruments for the small orchestra such as the drum-kit and the piano. Other instruments were brought in later by the musicians. If a hall had no seating of its own, this wasn't a problem. Flash Parade had its own stock of chairs. All of the "props" needed for the night's performance, were assembled together with the "78 rpm records" for the sound effects and incidental music. Chic had constructed a portable switchboard with dimmers and various switches and sockets including a second record-player. So everything was to hand.

All of these various props and technical materials were still in the cottage in Bruree when I first began to renovate it many years ago. Initially, I attempted to renovate all of these various items but as space was limited in the cottage it didn't prove practicable in the end. Instead of attempting to renovate everything I made sketches of these articles as they were then constructed and then dismantled them. For its time, the switchboard was quite sophisticated and also proved very compact for travelling. The large wood-mounted poster of my grandmother in her top-hat-and-tails was placed in the hallway or just inside the main door. This piece of memorabilia dates from the Twenties or early Thirties and is still in my possession – it continues to be a prominent feature of my cottage's interior.

Chic Kay aged about 10 with his musical instruments – c. 1942

Costumes for the performances had been sorted, ironed and hung up, in the dressing room. During our days on the road, there was no such as separate dressing rooms in most venues. So everybody just lumped in together and no-one took a blind bit of notice as to what stage of undress anyone else was in. They were too busy; they had a job to do, especially in the variety section of the show, where all the acts and sketches were moved on and off the stage at lightning speed. Never was this more apparent than on one particular night when there were two (rival) feuding families in the audience. Everything seemed to be going well until someone from one of these families passed a remark. One word led to another – and before you knew it - all hell had broken loose. There was a sudden charge up through the audience towards the dressing room as the front door was blocked off…Actors and players stood there in puzzlement as the screaming horde rushed past them and out the back door. Bemused, the players got back to "changing for the next act" and continued the show to wild applause!!

The only occasion I heard Granny Vic use the term "fit-up" was for when we did a "run-out". This occurred on those occasions when the hall we were playing in was needed for something else – in these instances we would do a "run-out" to another venue close by. The "set-up" would not be as "robust" or as detailed in this case as it would normally be in a more established venue. The show would be tailored to suit whatever stage set was available at that particular location – i.e. normally it would involve one roll drop, one set of tabs etc. Vic always felt that the term "fit-up" diminished the huge amount of work which went into the mounting of her show, and if the reactions of the audiences were anything to go by, she was not alone in this way of thinking…

For us children, Christmas on tour was a great time. Firstly, we got to "go to Dublin" to see the wonderful lights and to stay with our "other" Nana and Grand-dad – we also got great presents from an aunt in America. The large box which arrived every year unveiled a host of goodies. I used to get the most wonderful frocks, trimmed with "Broderie Anglaise", lovely colours – full-skirted and pretty. One early summer I had at least two dozen of these dresses which I wore every day to whichever school I was attending that week. To my mortification the weather turned nasty, so I had to go to school in my "normal" get-up: i.e. big woolly jumper, tartan skirt, grey woollen socks and a good pair of stout brogues!! By the time the good weather returned, it was time to leave and I was completely fed-up…! Given the compact nature of our caravan, each Christmas we had to sort out some of our toys for distribution by the local priest to the "needy" children of the parish. This always irritated us – having to give away our possessions. Of course, it made perfect sense to do this. On a purely practical level, we would have needed an articulated truck to transport all of the toys we had collected over the years. It was this, together with meeting the actress Billie Morton which led to my squirrel-like habit of hoarding things!! As a child, Billie would come to the show with her parents in Skerries, County Dublin. Having an early talent for entertaining, she did wicked impersonations of my grandmother –much to Vic's delight. During the daytime – Billie brought her dolls – *all* of them – which to me seemed like dozens. We would play with them on the verandah of our caravan, which was always used in the summer months. I really wished I'd had a collection like hers, and decided there and then, that one day, I too would have lots and lots of dolls!! Many dolls adorn my cottage now, including one which my grandmother gave to my mother when I was born. This is a German-made all-rubber doll with glass eyes, and dressed in a costume made with fabrics for the show. I often wonder if Billie kept any of her dolls...In Vic's caravan there was a doll on one of the walls that I'd always wished to have. Dark-skinned with long black hair, her costume consisted of a Hawaiian shirt, complete with diamante jewellery. Sadly, after my grandmother died, I never did get that doll. My love of dolls caught the attention of another family friend...the hypnotist Paul Goldin. When touring the country, we met him often and I always found him to be a kind and charming man. Once we went to one of his shows and he told the audience that they were going to meet his "new girlfriend". He pointed to me and told me to stand and "take a bow"...I did so, blushing furiously...well, eight-year old girls tend to do that...One afternoon, the family met him for afternoon tea. Afterwards he insisted on taking Ken and me to a toyshop, somewhere in Henry Street, in Dublin. I chose a lovely doll (which I still have. He also sent me a "Geisha" doll from Japan, but it never arrived....got lost in the postal system somewhere...!

Granny Vic was delighted to have a girl as her first grandchild, as she could now get to do a little spoiling. I learnt a lot from her, and she in turn couldn't resist "showing off" my perceived "skills". When visitors come to the wagon, I was to show everyone how I could "do the splits" – to rapturous and indulgent applause from the assembled guests...She had often wanted me to go to England to visit her family...but my mother was having none of it!!

My brother, on the other hand, had learned on that "Ma", as my Dad called Vic, was always good for a sub (which he never paid back!). So Ken would come "a-visiting" and was greeted with muttering that – "that little bugger's here for his 6d". When he sat there, saying very little, swinging his legs, and gazing at her with his big blue eyes – it was never too long before she gave in and gave him his 6d! – whereupon he'd gallop off with a quick "ta Gran", leaving her with a gratified smile on her face – and me tucking into her secret stash of chocolates!!

Even now, in my mind's eye, I can clearly see my grandmother's wagon and the details of her "palace on wheels' the satin brocade upholstery, the French polished wood; the glass corner unit – within it a silver tea service. There were Chinese ivory ornaments and crystal chandeliers. There was a beautiful glass-domed clock which Chic bought her for her 60th birthday; after which he promptly handed her the bill at a party given in her honour!! Under the table in the dining area, there was a china bowl with Brer rabbit characters on it, which Judy and Twinky her two yappy little dogs drank from; those dogs were spoilt rotten!! I have some small ebony elephants which stood on a shelf and a jar of sequins and a silver buckle bracelet – they are all I have from her caravan….In later years I would discover how valuable her collection really was. Unfortunately, however, it all disappeared over time – generally after being "borrowed" by people who had no entitlement to it…! After her death the caravan was completely cleared out by one of her so-called "friends".

Our first caravan, which was built by Dad and Frank Macari, was "compact" to say the least…It had a "galley" kitchen and a small loo. In the main room the table and seating could also be extended to form a double bed. There was a solid fuel stove in it and lots of storage space in the manner of all small wagons. Ken and I had the smallest bedroom – well bedroom was a bit of an overstatement. It was a large closet, big enough (just) to accommodate two small bunks. Years later, people would meet me with the words – "I used to remember you…when you slept in the wardrobe!" In the main room Dad had made glassed-in diorama's, depicting various scenes including an Irish cottage, a Hawaiian islan and a stagecoach being "attacked" by Indians. All of the miniature figures were painted by Dad, and all of the props and furniture were made by him also…

As we became older, the parents decided it was time to get a bigger wagon. We got a lovely brand-new *Saracen* caravan. To us kids, it was huge. It had beautifully-finished and built-in furniture. In the main room – which could be divided up – a double-bed came out of the wall. There was a loo, a shower, and a bigger galley kitchen – (than the one we had had in the previous wagon) – complete with pump-action taps. My mother was very proud of the red lino, which was polished every week. Considering the amount of muddy fields we tramped through on a regular basis, it was no mean feat to keep it pristine. That was one of the difficult aspects of touring – trying to keep your belongings clean and tidy – given the lack of space…oh, and yes – Ken and I got a bigger "wardrobe"!!

"On the Road" with our wagon and American car

One of the things Granny Vic insisted upon was that the area around the wagons was kept "spick-and-span". There was one time when she told someone on the show – to take some nappies off of a line because they hadn't been "properly" washed…there was an element of the "drill sergeant" about Vic…!!

As far as she was concerned, there was a standard to be kept – and that was the end of it. When you think of it – we had to get our water from the pumps which were dotted all over the countryside. We had a huge water tank we filled up in the caravan, which we used until we got to the next pump…no such thing as hooking up to a water supply then! We also had gas lamps in all of the rooms, and gas was also used for cooking. A solid fuel stove was used for heating. One had to be forever watchful, as all it took was one wrong move…and that's precisely what happened!! Ken and I cheated death…with a twist…

Chic serenades Vic outside the booth. Ken trying to join in on the action!

The show had started and there were people from Dublin who were visiting us. During the interval, my mother asked one of the women, "to put a couple of briquettes on the fire". This woman who could be a bit "dippy" at the best of times piled on a huge amount of briquettes and went back to the show. Unfortunately the chimney inside the airing cupboard, which was packed with clothes, was not insulated. The inevitable happened and it caught fire! Anyone who has seen a caravan go up in flames will know how quickly a fire can spread. Luckily for us, a cat who never went out at night and was ensconced in a neighbouring wagon – made such a racket that its owner spotted the flames and raised the alarm…All Ken and I remember is being grabbed from our bunks and being brought out to a gathering crowd – mother hysterical while people dowsed the flames…Our brave rescuer…was none other than Tex the Fire-eater!!

Patrickswell in County Limerick was another place where we had a "brush with death". It was a cold, wet day, but that didn't stop us kids from going out to play. Me and Ken were playing "shooting down planes" when everything went black. We had been behind our gran's big car when another car travelling towards Limerick took the bend to fast and smashed into our car, trapping me behind it. Ken had managed to jump clear – John Wayne fashion…When I came to, mother was trying to pull the car away as my foot was trapped under the wheel. She was soon joined by a group from the village who lifted the heavy car away from me…After a quick check-up, it was announced that I was fine again, if a little damp – as I'd been pushed into a hedge behind me. There had been talk of that hedge being replaced with a wall – but the weather had been too bad to build it… Having spent so many years touring with caravans and trucks – and being able to pack so much stuff into transportable spaces – I've used that knowledge since in my cottage in Bruree, County Limerick. From the built-in furniture, made by me, to the copious amount of shelving – there is no area that is not used to full capacity…People are always amazed at the sheer quantity of bric-a-brac that I have – I call it "caravan mentality" or solutions for small spaces! The cottage itself was little more than a roof and four walls when I decided to renovate it - having been divested of all costumes, props etc. – many years ago – again by people with no entitlement to them!

I have a saying - "poverty is a great designer"…having little money gives one time to think about doing the right thing! The cottage is still in accordance with its original architectural design and today, it houses what is left of the memorabilia from Granny Vic's show. I think she'd be proud of what I've done with what was once a simple "storage facility". I also had the cottage certified as a "listed building" [19]

---

[19] A "Listed Building" is one included in a statutory list of buildings of special architectural or historic interest as compiled by the local government in Ireland.

In 1962, Vic decided it was time "to close the show" and for a time we lived in Croom, County Limerick. We have cine-film of that period, film which is also in the RTE archives. Vic and Frank then moved to Drogheda in County Louth. During their latter years, they both continued to do "spots" in various shows and cabarets. Our branch of the family ended up moving to Bray, County Wicklow and then onto Shankill in County Dublin. Vic and Frank then also moved to Shankill – to be "near family" – which meant we got to see Vic every day. The one regret that I now have is that when I was a teenager I was too absorbed with my own life and so gradually got to see Vic less and less. One of the last times I spoke to her she was getting "tarted up" in true Showbiz spirit and I asked her where she was going…whereupon she promptly responded – "I am going to the weekly Old Folks Club entertain those old buggers". She was 86 years of age then!!

It was the first time I'd ever seen her use a mic…!

The whole family kept a hand in the entertainment business – what with variety shows, drama, and summer seasons – and in the 70s, Ken and I were in bands and on the disco scene…Once, in a Dublin night club named *Sloopys*, I was billed as "Vikki J. Go-Go Pet" - I have to stress that nightclubs then were far more innocent places than they are now!!
Ken became involved with radio in England while I later went into theatrical design make-up and costume…

We are both still involved with our "theatrical roots" and continue to enjoy what we do – him being big into the technical side of things – and me still carrying on the tradition of designing and making costumes, set design and theatrical make-up…and…making things out of nothing!! I have always been fascinated with my "Showbiz" background and regularly do tours/talks for visitors to my cottage. It is important to keep alive the memories of those hardworking, talented and undervalued artistes who entertained the masses under good…bad…and downright grotty conditions! -artistes who never lost their enthusiasm to enthral audiences with music, song, dance and acting.

Nous avons changé tout cela.
—Moliére

Vic as you've never seen her before!

Peter Piper's grave in Lismore, County Waterford. Inscribed with the opening notes of "Just a Song at Twilight"

OTHER SIDE OF THE FOOTLIGHTS:
AUDIENCE MEMORIES

…I remember when I was a little girl sometime in the early 1930s, my grandmother living in Belfast was very ill, and dying actually. So my older sister and my younger brother, both now deceased – went to Newcastle, County Down, with a house and every night she took us to the "Pierrots". This was a show on a sort of a grandstand on the pier. There was a Punch and Judy Show, a line of Tap dancers and the usual comedian and stooge. I think they went on performing for about one and a half hours…
—E.L., County Dublin

…Your letter stirred happy memories childhood and teenage years in the 30s and 40s when I was an ardent and devoted fan of the touring companies, who visited our village in Westmeath, their names still come to mind, viz: Carrickford's, which was top-class with superb actors; Mrs. O'Shea; Uncle Joe's and many others come to mind. Mrs. O'Shea was principal and leading lady of O'Shea's and had been a handsome lady in - still retaining striking good looks. She was courageous and daring presenting *Gone with the Wind* and playing Scarlet herself with aplomb and to our unsophisticated but fiercely critical assessment, not in the least incongruous. Her husband was a believable Rhett Butler. He was a chain smoker and in a production of *Dracula*, playing the eponymous role as he lay dying gasping for breadth, with a fag in his mouth and a dagger imbedded in his chest as he expired.

And then there was uncle Joe's, a strictly family-only employer. The phrase "With Uncle Joe's" being "out or work" or resting.

The travelling players in those days performed and rendered a great service in rural Ireland, during a period of famine entertainment-wise, which is impossible to visualise now – filling a great gap for cultural and mental stimuli. Their visits were eagerly and impatiently anticipated; once the posters were on the billboards, the days were counted off! Opening Night! We were on a high of feverish expectation of the delights to come – comedy-tragedy-whatever-all hit the target, with perhaps a bias towards tragedy; one became totally involved, identifying so completely with the suffering and trauma depicted vividly before one's young eyes, a cathartic

experience as the curtain descended, the performance was finished/over, but not in one's head, where it was repeated and retained along the road home, all night, next day and next week.
—P.L., London

…My parents had a "Hall/Cinema" in Miltown Malbay during the forties through the late fifties where some of the travelling shows would play for a week or two before moving onto the next venue. Needless to say as a young fellow we hung around them during the day doing odd jobs such as putting posters up or acting as general dogs-bodies in order to get free admission to the night's performances. I suppose that this gave us some insight as to how they operated.

…the only one who had a show in the all was Vic Loving, in fact herself and Chic Kay had a flaming row and broke up while in Miltown. However there were others…who are worthy of mention… particularly: Anew McMaster, The Shannon Players, Louis Dalton, Jim Parks, Ben Bono and a magic show where the magician was called "Bennon". This show had a live lion which the first time any of us had seen one!

McFaddens had a travelling cinema with a new episode of a serial every night. Needless to say, there was strong opposition from ourselves and when they moved on, sighs of relief were released all-round.
—M.H., Limerick.

I spent the first ten year of my life in Bruree, County Limerick (1936-46) – my father was a National teacher there. I have distinct memories of some of the shows you mention - Vic Loving in particular – being performed in the village hall – I can recall the following:
1. Plays being performed in the hall in Bruree, in particular "Murder in the Red Barn" and "Night Must Fall".
2. A Singing Duet, Phil Mount and his wife, Betty.
3. Harry Bailey had an act during which which he played the violin.

I cannot recall which touring shows contained the above acts. However, I am certain of our touring show, Bill Costello was its leader. He played "Al Jolson" singing *Sonny Boy*, I played the part (a silent one) of Sonny Boy at his knee. The name *Taylor* keeps recurring in my thoughts. Why all of these shows visited a small place like Bruree, equidistant from two larger towns, Kilmallock and Charleville, I do not know…
—L.R., Dublin.

…your letter brought back sweet memories of many enjoyable nights out at the Vic Loving shows in Rush, Co. Dublin. Like many Dublin families in the 1950-1960 years, we moved out to a rented thatched cottage in Rush for a month or two every summer. We went for seventeen years in total. They were very basic – outdoor facilities etc. and a tap at the front door – these little inconveniences didn't deter holiday fun in any way. Most of the Rush farmers gave work to the Dublin children over eight years – helping to pick tomatoes, pick peas and sort out bulbs - Dutch families had bought land in Rush and established bulb growing to supply the Dublin Market with flowers. The money gained at this work was saved and later spent - going every night if possible to the shows. We watched them put up the bill-boards, erect the tent – it was the topic of conversation for the week! Shows like *East Lynn, the Story of Bernadette*, cowboy stories etc. "Marie Keane" was a native of Rush where she was in residence as Mrs Mulvey, Main Street. She had a son John who lived there and played along with us as a child. She was an "Abbey Actress" – Mrs. Kennedy of Castle Ross was another of her roles on Radio. She performed there to "rave reviews". Andrew McMaster also performed and other Abbey friends of Maud Kean. Andrew McMaster also performed and other Abbey friends of Marie Keane. Mr. Golden etc. helped out. There were always full houses! Patrons sat on Forum's – long benches in the canvas tent. Skerries (six miles north of Rush also hosted the shows and at Red Island Holiday camp there. Just flicking through the rough selection from *Sunday Miscellany* 1995-2000 I spotted "Life upon the Wicked Stage" by Ted Goodman. He mentioned acting in *The Informer* by Liam O'Flaherty. Others like *Peg O' My Heart, Maria Marten and Murder in the Red Barn* were also acted.
—M.K., Co. Meath.

My late father Jim Howley was in digs as they were called long ago with Agnew McMaster's mother in Dublin. Jim was an electrician so he was asked by Agnew to be part of his traveling show. They were in some small town in the west of Ireland performing and one of the Artists became ill so dad (Jim) was told – "you are on tonight". He spent all the day learning his one line, went into make-up, put on his costume and went on stage and opened his mouth to deliver his line and he said to me – "M… nothing came out." He often told me this story but my mother never heard it.

Now my mother and her friend Bridie (now deceased) never missed a show in the Parochial Hall in Ballinasloe when McFaddens performed – notably, *Noreen Ban* etc. They were always in the front row and always cried at the appropriate time. They were great memories…
—MHJ, Ballinasloe, Galway.

…The summer of 1955 I was staying at my grandmother's in Skerries and Vic Loving arrived in town. The performance started at 8 pm and started at 8 pm with song and dance – local talent would take part i.e. singing whatever songs were popular at the time. After the intermission a play was put on which to me was to me was pure magic equal to – if not superior to Dublin theatre which I would have been particular with. One particular performance was "Murder in the Old Red Barn". Chic Kay being Vic Loving's son and the wife were the main stars – admission was 1 shilling - a considerable amount in the time. After Skerries they would travel to Ballinasloe and during the winter they performed in small theatres in Dublin. They never returned after 1955. I recall seeing Vic Loving on the Late Late during the 70s and she could still sing and dance. My husband recalls a traveling show coming to his area called The *Reillys*…his recollections are vague…*Flash Parade* was the name Vic Loving's show went under. Every morning on a well-known notice board the title of that night's play would be given. In those pre-television days, the tent would be full to capacity.
—M.M., Swords, Dublin.

…I am going back over 70 years in my recollections of the "Fit-Ups". The shows that I love to remember are Vic Loving and her husband Peter Piper and son "Chicago Kid". Peter Piper is buried in the cemetery here in Lismore (County Waterford). George Daniels, must have been the last to visit here, where he set up in the Showgrounds under canvas. Another show company was Carrickfords who played straight plays followed by variety. Then we had visits from Gerry Brodbin, again with straight plays such as *Murder in the Red* Barn and *The Road Back.* He had beautiful stage curtains and his company were the first to play in a hall here, a converted saw-mill - some time in the '40s. He ran a competition for the naming of the "new" hall, which was given the name "The HappyDrome". The play was followed by variety….you mentioned the Creagh Brothers – I wonder if they were neighbours of ours in this street. – John and Bob. They were interested in music from their boyhood. Bob eventually built a horsedrawn caravan in their garden – this was during the war. My brother shod the horse, with rubbers fitted for the tar road but the first evening he tethered the animal, he broke loose and made his way back home!...other traveling shows who visited the area included *Dobells* and *Anew McMaster*…
—P.V. Lismore, County Waterford.

…My father Bryan Guinness, 2nd Lord Moyne was a poet, wrote two plays and went to the theatre as much as he could, taking the older children with him. He loved the west of Ireland and took a cottage every summer, somewhere in Connemara I think it was; we travelled in an old Ford V8 with a goat in the dog compartment to provide "safe" milk for a succession of babies - we were a family of 11. We sat on wooden benches in the tent with the grass under our feet. There was an hour or two's wait for the pubs to shut and the audience to emerge when, in case we fled I suppose, we were entertained by of a girl of about fourteen, playing a drum. *Lady Oranmore's Secret* is the only name of a play I can remember, an account of our cousin of that name. When I married and came to live in Co. Kildare the Fit-ups were in Maynooth and Celbridge, not in a hall but in a tent with a grass floor. People used to change for dinner in the 50s and we always rushed through the meal to get to the play, the men in black ties. I should be going to this this entertainment today, with my grandchildren, if it still existed.
—D.G., Leixlip Castle, Leixlip, Co. Kildare.

...During the 1950s I lived on Valentia Island, and at the time there was no bridge to the mainland. Everything had to come by ferry, which was a smallish boat owned by a Murphy family. When there was a large cargo - such as on fair days or when a car was being brought across - a second boat was towed across. One of the more dramatic, and eagerly awaited, cargoes would be the sets, props and everything else when the travelling shows visited the island, and we all, as youngsters, would lend a hand or, more likely, get in the way as the cargo was loaded at Renard on the mainland and unloaded at Knight's Town Pier and brought up to the hall by the horse and cart. I'm afraid the scene was so commonplace at the time, nobody thought to take a photograph. A travelling show that frequently visited was Jimmy Robertson's. They would peform in the local hall, St. Derarca's in Knight Town, for a period of a week, different shows every night. There was East Lynne; Murder in the Old Red Barn (Maria Martin); The Bard of Armagh; Abdication; Treasure Island; The Face at the Window; some others which I do not remember, but most of them had exotic costumes and sword fights. Jimmy Robertson was a small, dapper Scotsman, and at every night the shows would open with Jimmy on his ukulele singing "Rolling Round the World". He normally played the villain, but he also played the Bard of Armagh, dramatically dying on stage with "And forget - (Gasp) - that you ever heard of - (Gasp - the Bard of Armagh." His daughter (I forget her name) played the female leads, and occasionally the male Juvenile - she was Jim Hawkins. She was married to the romantic lead, Victor Acers, who also played the piano accordion and sang - "Goodbye" from "White Horse Inn" and "Harbour Lights" were his usual hits. Others came and went, and the child in "East Lynne" was always played by "A Local Boy" - on one occasion, my brother Denis had the "starring" role.

There was no electricity, so everything was done by oil lamps. No fire regulations then! They managed several scene changes in impossible conditions, and in the Red Barn they even managed a dream scene at the rear of the stage in addition to the main scene - remarkable as the stage can't have been more than 10' deep (Half a dozen large tables held together). As far as I remember, the price for children was 6d, and there was the obligatory raffle. What became of Jimmy and his troupe I do not know - I believe they spent some time in Dundalk in the Oriel cinema, but subsequently? Other troupes came to the island, Dorothy Daniel's is a name I remember, but the only group I remember for their shows was Jimmy Robertson's......
—A.G., Peake, Coachford, Co. Cork.

...Your letter stirred happy memories childhood and teenage years in the 30s and 40s when I was an ardent and devoted fan of the touring companies, who visited our village in Westmeath, their names still come to mind, viz: Carrickford's, which was top-class with superb actors; Mrs. O'Shea; Uncle Joe's and many others come to mind. Mrs. O'Shea was principal and leading lady of O'Shea's and had been a handsome lady in - still retaining striking good looks. She was courageous and daring presenting *Gone with the Wind* and playing Scarlet herself with aplomb and to our unsophisticated but fiercely critical assessment, not in the least incongruous. Her husband was a believable Rhett Butler. He was a chain smoker and in a production of *Dracula*, playing the eponymous role as he lay dying gasping for breadth, with a fag in his mouth and a dagger imbedded in his chest as he expired. And then there was uncle Joe's, a strictly family-only employer. The phrase "With Uncle Joe's" being "out or work" or resting. The travelling players in those days performed and rendered a great service in rural Ireland, during a period of famine entertainment-wise, which is impossible to visualize now – filling a great gap for cultural and mental stimuli. Their visits were eagerly and impatiently anticipated; once the posters were on the billboards, the days were counted off! Opening Night! We were on a high of feverish expectation of the delights to come – comedy-tragedy-whatever-all hit the target, with perhaps a bias towards tragedy; one became totally involved, identifying so completely with the suffering and trauma depicted vividly

before one's young eyes, a cathartic experience as the curtain descended, the performance was finished/over, but not in one's head, where it was repeated and retained along the road home, all night, next day and next week.
—P.L., London.

…My parents had a "Hall/Cinema" in Miltown Malbay during the forties through the late fifties where some of the travelling shows would play for a week or two before moving onto the next venue. Needless to say as a young fellow we hung around them during the day doing odd jobs such as putting posters up or acting as general dogs-bodies in order to get free admission to the night's performances. I suppose that this gave us some insight as to how they operated.

   …the only one who had a show in the all was Vic Loving, in fact herself and Chic Kay had a flaming row and broke up while in Miltown. However there were others…who are worthy of mention… particularly: Anew McMaster, The Shannon Players, Louis Dalton, Jim Parks, Ben Bono and a magic show where the magician was called "Bennon". This show had a live lion which the first time any of us had seen one! McFaddens had a travelling cinema with a new episode of a serial every night. Needless to say, there was strong opposition from ourselves and when they moved on, sighs of relief were released all-round.
—M.H. Limerick.

…I am 93 years old now but well remember the travelling shows from England that visited Skerries every summer. Many people living in North Dublin went to Skerries for their holidays and enjoyed the concerts given by these travelling shows from England. A platform would be erected in front of which would be chairs and for which there would be a charge. Many people just stood around and enjoyed a free concert. During the interval a member of the cast would come around with a collecting box for contributions. There was never any trouble at these open-air concerts which were part of the summer and much enjoyed by many people, both young and old.
—E.L., Dublin

…I remember the Daniels and O'Shea's visiting Drumkeerin, County Leitrim in the early forties. It was in 1941 when I was eleven years old. I went to see *Murder in the Red Barn* and *East Lynne.* I will tell you of an incident; my father was the local Garda Sergeant (Sergeant Matt Gallagher) at the time. I was asked by my mother to give him a message, we lived next door to the Garda Station. As I entered, the Garda Station's day-room and my father was speaking to Mr. Daniels, I passed the message to my Dad and then Mr. Daniels asked – "How many children have you?" and my Dad said – "Seven". Mr. Daniels then took a card from his pocket and wrote, "Let these seven children in free, Sergeant's children". I took the card and presented it to the lady in the box office; she did not bat an eye when she read the card. "Let these seventeen children in free – Sergeant's children", she said. I had rounded up all my schoolfriends and entered 17! Two of these schoolfriends I met this year in Drumkeerin in July, after fifty years. When the Daniels left we decided to act our own shows giving the proceeds to Saint Teresa's Penny Dinners in Dublin – the most we made was seventeen shillings. I married a Guard and while stationed in different areas

...During the forties, fifties and early sixties...touring companies of actors and variety artists played an important part providing entertainment in Ashford during this period. At least three different companies included Ashford amongst their venues on their countrywide tours. *The Macks* were perhaps the best known of these companies. They first appeared in the pavilion in Ballinalea in the 1920s. An Irish company based in Dublin, they specialized in staging full-length plays with a small number of variety acts to fill out the evening's entertainment. The most popular plays were East Lynne, The Robe, Murder in the Red Barn, and Napoleon and Josephine. The owner and the leader of the company, Mr. Mack always played the part of Napoleon, his favourite role. The variety acts appearing with the Macks were usually talented, and one of them, an accordionist, had appeared on the London stage. *The Macks* last appeared in Ashford in 1942. In the 1930s, another traveling company, *The Tower Mascots*, appeared in the pavilion in Ballinalea. They also put on full-length plays supplemented with a few variety acts. A Scottish company *The Millers* played the hall in Ballinalea on a number of occasions in the late twenties. They staged variety concerts only. A raffle for a large range of household goods which were displayed in the hall was one of the great attractions of their visits to Ashford. The traveling cinema provided another popular form of entertainment. During the 1930s, the *Irish-American Talkiedrome* presented film shows in a film tent erected outside the pavilion in Ballinalea. Another traveling cinema known as *The Odeon* presented film shows in the dancehall of *Bel-Air Hotel* and in Cunniam's pavilion in the centre of the village...

—from D. Fitzpatrick – *Entertainment in Ashford 1900-1950* pp.26-27.

…My own memories are of "Maria Martin" and "Murder at the Red Barn", and how we cheered when the villain William Corder got his come-uppance, not to mention the old favourite, Mrs. Wood'-s "East Lynne". I recall also "The Tears of an Old Irish Mother", "Noreen Bawn" and the humorous "Charley's Aunt". The shows all had the same format, the opening "here we are again" or "no business like show business", the funny sketches (all shows had their funny men), the raffle, the main play and the final funny sketch to send us home in good spirits. Then of course there was the Talent Competition where the locals sang, danced or played an instrument, and got whittled down to the final night. Usually the judging was done by the amount of applause the audience gave to each competitor. L sang in several of these contests and indeed won 2/6 in a children's one singing "Forever and ever my heart will be true"....my dear mother was a great fan of the shows and used to marvel at the acting, the singing and the beauty of the girls. I wonder if the girls had "admirers" who followed them around….
—D.C. Bromley, Kent

…I was living in Mountmellick, Co.   Laois, in 1945 or '46 and Vic Loving had a tent in Felix Paly's field,   which at that time was the Road Show ground. It was not a 3-pole tent like today's Circus tents, but it was quite large and she put on a different show for six nights. The show I went to was   'Cinderella' and I have   to say that before or since I have not   seen a better show. She was   a cracking   singer with   a tremendous repertoire. I can see her now in my mind's eye, - she played the Mother and the Prince; Frank Macari, the great Piano Accordionist and Vic's son Chic played the Ugly Sisters. All the rest I can see in my mind as though it were yesterday: Chic with his 'Holy - Poly' stunt. He would invite members of the audience to try it - a time-filler while the scene was   being changed. Macari played some great music…The costumes were lavish and the whole show was a howl from start to finish. I was somewhere near the front row and I think it only cost two bob (10p). There was no amplification but Vic did not need any; she could be heard out in the street.
—(T.G.) Staffordshire, England

…there never was, never has been or never will be another 'Vic1. I was born and reared in Bunclody, Co. Wexford and it was in Co. tfexford 1 first got to know Vic, and I travelled everywhere I could possibly go to be at her nightly performances. Her show was entitled 'The Flash Parade1, She herself was a great actress, singer, etc., and I can still remember her

beautiful blue dress and parasol when she u^ed to sing "Alice Blue Gown". I remember her son Brian and also Frank Macari who was a wizard on the accordion. More of the cast were: Jimmy and Dolly Stone, Cliff Bolton and his wife, and some very nice girls   I still talk to people about her - Vic - and the wonderful performances she would put on - my eldest daughter remembers going with me to the performances as a child. She is now fifty years of age and I myself will be seventy next year. It was around 1939 and after when I knew Vic…Oh! How I loved   all   the travelling   shows. The Carrickford Productions, Jimmy O'Dea and Harry O'Donovan, Anew Mc Master. I could go on and on...with best wishes from one who had great admiration and respect for your dear grandmother.
—(V.H.), Athlone, Co. Westmeath

I read with interest your letter about your grandmother Vic Loving. Her shows in Skerries, Co. Dublin in the 1950's were 'MAGIC'. I recall a man named Macari who played   an accordion and an actor named Kay who was on the show. I worked for   'Autocars' (Ford) in Dublin in the '50's and I remember your grandmother bought a Ford Zephyr and she always looked after us when we   serviced it for her. Reading your letter in the papers is certainly a 'Blast from the past' for me; it brings back many memories.
—(N.S.) Dublin

Some Memories of the Travelling Road Shows
by Jim McCarthy

Many are the happy memories I have stored up of the many travelling drama and variety shows which came to our Town every year. I well remember the first of those great shows I attended when I was nine or ten years old. That was around the year 1930 and the place everyone headed for was the old Cinema Hall, at the lower or northern end of the Main Street in Buttevant Co. Cork. The show was billed for some weeks before and was known to all as "Miss Vic Loving's Flash Parade". The show was run and directed by the great lady herself, Vic Loving, whose real name was Mrs Victoria. On that first visit of mine 60-odd years ago the panto Miss Vic Loving presented was "Dick Whittington and his Cat". Until the great Vic gave up the shows and went into retirement I never missed one of the performances in Buttevant and Mitchelstown where I later went to live.

ANEW MCMASTER AT PAROCHIAL HALL CHARLEVILLE
When I grew older and became the owner of a bicycle I attended all the great shows that were presented yearly at the Parochial Hall in Charleville, Co. Cork. We had the great Anew McMaster, The Shannon Players and The Carrickfords who also put on great shows. One member of that family is very well known today to thousands of Television viewers as Stephen Brennan of Glenroe.

BAMBOOZELUM
Another great attraction in my young days was "Bamboozelum" - the great conjuror who supplied all the men of the parish with braces from an empty shoe box. Bamboozelum could change into a dozen different suits in as many seconds to the delight of all of us young lads.

THE BAILEYS, GABY AND UNCLE GADGET
Baileys show was another show we looked forward to every year when we had pains in our sides laughing at the great comedian, Gaby, who was also a fine singer. In that fine show there was also Uncle Gadget, a fine performer on the piano-accordion.

THE BEN-BONO SHOW
Another show that came to Buttevant, County Cork, in my young days was a show run by a gentleman who called himself Ben-Bono. I never knew his real name but in that show I saw an act for the first time which later became well known to thousands of television viewers. It was Eugene Lambert and Finnegan of "Wanderly Wagon" fame. On that great show was a great performer on the Banjo named Bert Patterson. I often thought of Bert since and where he went to. I hope he is still with us. Bert Patterson was a fine singer also and one of his songs I remember still was called "The Leprechaun".

GEORGE DANIELS AND HIS GREAT SHOW
The George Daniels Company were among the greatest of the travelling shows. I never missed a performance of the Daniels show when they played to packed houses in the Old British Legion Hall in Buttevant long ago. George Daniels was a personal friend of mine and I had a drink with him in Clongibbon House in Mitchelstown, when he last came to that town on a visit to two local Amusement caterers - Davy Whelan and John Fry. The last time I spoke to George Daniels was at Emmet Place in Cork City, when he was lending a hand at a street carnival. The world is poorer with the passing of such great men as George Daniels. The famous ballad

"Noreen Bawn" was written by Goerge Daniels and when he produced the play of that name the whole audience was brought to tears when the lights were lowered and the lonely widow knelt beside the grave - "In a graveyard in Tirconnell".

I will never forget the drama, song, music, and comedy of the great Daniel's show. In those years Bracey Daniels, the father of George, played in the show. He was a fine performer and sang some good comic songs to our delight. A few lines of the song I can still remember: "When the old torn cat, played spoons upon the mat" With the Ginger-haired Cat next Door'. George Daniels spent his last years in Belfast.

DERMOT DENNEHY AND THE GLENSIDE PLAYERS
Dermot Dennehy grew up in the town of Charleville, County Cork, in a place called Newtown Barry, on the Kilmallock Road, just across from the Golden Vale Cheese factory. I knew Dermot well as a young lad growing up and he always had a flair for comedy, singing and step-dancing. Away back in the late thirties and early forties when World War II was at its height, a couple of local lads got together, organised some talent and began to hold concerts in the Parochial Hall in Charleville. The late 3&£h Russell, later to become Br. Stephen, an Alexian Brother, and a chap known as Doc Daly, were two of the organisers. I attended the first concert and one of the principal characters was my friend Dermot Dennehy. He sang, danced, and acted in short sketches to the delight of all, especially people like myself who know him personally. Thirty years or so later when I had long left Buttevant and the Charleville district and was living in Mitchelstown, I attended a travelling show. One day I saw some caravans and a tent being erected in Davy Whelan's Circus field, just across the road from where I live. I took a closer look and saw a poster being displayed which read. "Glenside Players" performing nightly for one week. That night I walked across the road, purchased a ticket and took a seat in the tent. Surprise, surprise, and what a surprise when the show started and who should hop out on the stage dressed in a suit of many colours only my lifelong friend Dermot Dennehy, from Charleville. Dermot had married a lovely lady named Kay, they started their own show and went on tour. Some few years later I was shocked to hear of Dermot Dennehy's death. In the "Glenside Show" was a fine singer from Co. Limerick named Sonny Coll. Somebody told me that Sonny later gave up the stage and worked as a rep.

THE END OF THE ROAD

Dermot Dennehy and the Glenside Players were the last of the travelling road shows that came to this town where I now live. The box on the stand in the corner of the room and the pubs opening on Sunday nights with ballad sessions and dancing, sounded the death knell of the travelling shows. In those happy days of the dance and the fit-ups we looked forward to a show and we went off whistling happily and came home with a clearer mind. We knew nothing about vandalism or any of the present day violence or unrest. If we had the few bob for the show we were the happiest lads and lassies in the world. You could throw the old bike and the bicycle pump and lamp in any corner of the town and if you did not come to pick it up until that day week, it would still be where you left it.. I often try to tell the young lads growing up about the great Vic Loving and Annie Dalton who became better known as Minnie of The Riordan's'. Her stage husband Batty Brennan, who, as Frank O'Donovan, often brought his show to the old Hall, known locally as 'The Kinema1 in Buttevant long ago, and who wrote the great ballad "Sitting On The Bridge Below The Town".

The young lads of today have no interest only in all the rock-stars that daub our television screens. An old man said to me lately that 'the greatest curse that struck Ireland since the Famine was the fake-a-me-gig in the corner'. Maybe he's not too far wrong, as it definitely helped to bring about the demise of the travelling road shows.

OTHER SHOWS: OTHER PROS

Some of the Irish Travelling Shows

Bohemian Players
Frank O'Donovan Show
McKenzie Show Stars
Shaw Company
Mrs Dalton's Irish Players
Colm and Edna McCormack Show
Vic Loving's Flash Parade
Livingstone Company
Ben Bono's Company
The Starlight Players
Barrett Company
Val Vousden Company
The Jabs
Herman and Bernie O'Shea's Company
Mark Wynnes Company
Harry Lyntons Hippodrome
Histella International Theatre Show
Carrie Hennessy-Norman Moane
Brefni O'Rourke's Company
The Mogador Company
Good Companions
Carrickfords Company
Garryowen Players
Mac's Show Stars
Jock and Alma Greer Show
Percy Holmshaw Company
Jimmy O'Dea Show
Anew McMaster Show
Peter Pipers Palladiums
The Harry Martins Show
Quigley and Traynor Show
Pat McEntee Players
Denis Murrays Company

The Leeside Players
Donald and Francis Hayden Show
Jim Parkes Company
Jack Reno's Company
The Glenside Players
Richard Carrickford Company
Dorothy Daniels Show
Dublin Repertory Theatre
Ronald Lee's Company
Dorothy Grafton Company
Courtneys Road Show
Eamonn Gallaghers Company
Derek Cobbe Show
Martin Crosby
Moylan's Hippodrame
Genesis Troupe
Eddie Mac's Company
Ray Mirth's Company
The Civic Players
The McFadden show
Brendan Smith Company
Great Bamboozelam
The Struan-Robertson Players
Alcona Family Show
R.J. Hope
Neilus O'Connell Promotions
Percy Morton Wright
The Unity Players
W.E. Dobell's Company
Dusky Dan
Hawthorn Players
Tara Players
The George Daniels Show
McCormacks Mumming Booth
Tara
Bailey's Road Shoe
Geoffrey Kendall Company
Mrs. Walshe's Show Stalls
The Shannon Players
The Moronis
Violet Mayons Company

The Civic Players
Mark Wynnes Company
The Starlight Players

Harry Tate - (1872-1940)

Harry Tate was a Scottish comedian who worked in both music hall and in film. Born Ronald Macdonald Hutchinson in 1872, he worked for sugar refiners Henry Tate and Sons, taking to the stage, where he adopted the name of his former employers as his stage surname. Tate made his debut at the *Oxford* in 1895, and his forte was as an impresario or impressionist – i.e. undertaking impressions of such well-known performers as Dan Leno, Eugene Stratton and George Robey. Success came to his door with a comedy sketch entitled *Motoring* where he played the part of a new car owner, (a chauffeur) who consistently fails to get his car started so as to take his son to college. Other sketches of his included *Running an Office* and *Billiards and Fishing*, *Selling a Car* and *Golfing*. Several of Tate's catch phrases became very popular in Britain during the 1930s including "Goodbye-eee", "How's yer Father" (used as a "diversion" when he was unable to answer a question) and "I don't think", - the latter phrase used in a sarcastic fashion - (as in "He's a nice chap – I don't think"). Tate also used his bushy moustache as a vehicle for comedy, employing it to express a range of emotions- depending on how he twitched it or moved it. The phrase "Harry Tate" itself entered the English language as slang when it was used as a knickname for the RAF R.E.8 biplane. When used as an adjective, this phrase meant "amateur" or "incompetent". It also entered English rhyming slang. In cockney rhyming slang for example, the phrase "Harry Tate" could mean either a "plate" or "worried" (from the expression "in a state"). Harry Tate died in 1940 from injuries he suffered during one of the many air raids that was the London Blitz. His son, Ronnie, acted with his father's company from the end of the First World War onwards and kept the act going for some years after Harry died – performing as 'Harry Tate Junior'.

Harry Tate: Filmography

Her First Affair - 1932
Happy - 1934
Midshipman Easy - 1935
Hyde Park Corner - 1935
Keep Your Seats Please - 1936

Wings of the Morning – 1937

Dan Leno - (1860 - 1904)

Dan Leno born George Wild Galvin (1860 - 1904) was an English music hall comedian whose act typically revolved around cockney humour and dressing up as a pantomime dame.Dan was born in Somers Town, London the son of comedian John Galvin and his wife, vocalist Louisa Dutton, appearing as the music hall entertainers Mr and Mrs Johnny Wilde. Dan was the youngest of four children, the eldest Jack, his other brother, Henry and sister, Frances. In 1864, he made his début at the Cosmotheca Music Hall in Paddington when he was billed as Little George, the Infant Wonder, Contortionist and Posturer. His father died in 1864, at the age of 37 and by 1866, his mother remarried the comedian Will Leno, moving to Liverpool, leaving Henry and Frances with the Galvin family in London.

Dan and his brother appeared as The Brothers Leno - Champion Dancers, and the family toured the halls throughout the north of England, Scotland and Ireland. In his late teens he developed a solo act. Leno remained small in his adult life reaching only 5ft 3ins. He was a very good clog dancer and entered a competition in 1880, at the Princess's Music Hall in Leeds. The competition was supposed to be rigged, but he overcame the obstacles to become World Champion Clog Dancer and win a gold and silver belt weighing 44.5 oz (1.26 kg). His biographer, J.Hickory Wood (1859-1925) described his act thus: He danced on the stage; he danced on a pedestal; he danced on a slab of slate; he was encored over and over again; but throughout his performance, he never uttered a word.

In 1883 Leno met Sarah Lydia Reynolds, a comedy singer, they married at St. George's Church, Hulme, in Manchester the following year and the first of six children was born, Georgina. The family moved back to London and Leno began his success with a new act, featuring comedy patter, dancing and song. He appeared at three music halls in one night, the Middlesex (Drury Lane), the Forester's (Mile End) and Gatti's-in-the-Road. He set about creating various comedic characters, including dames, a police officer, a Spanish bandit, a fire-fighter, and a hairdresser. He would begin with one verse of a song, then enter into his monologue with the audience, particularly the You know Mrs. Kelly?... routine — these increased his fame and he shot to 'top of the bill'. In the 1880s he became probably the most popular music hall act in England, performing in up to 20 shows a night. In 1896 he was hired by Augustus Harris, manager at

Drury Lane to appear in pantomime productions that included Jack and the Beanstalk, Babes in the Wood and Mother Goose. In virtually all of these production he played the dame to Marie Lloyd's principle girl. At this time, the pantomime would play continuously from the Christmas season to Easter.

He proved to be so popular that he even entertained Edward VII at Sandringham, later earning him the nickname the King's Jester. In 1902, under the strain of continuous performance, Leno suffered a mental breakdown and died soon after at the age of 43. "General Paralysis Of The Insane", a common euphemism for syphilis, was listed on his death certificate; Leno, however, was more likely suffering from a brain tumor which had caused his behaviour to become increasingly erratic. His funeral was a public occasion, the biggest funeral for an actor or comedian since the death of David Garrick. The Times wrote To find anything like a close parallel to his style we should probably have to go back to the Italian commedia dell'arte. Dan Leno is buried in Lambeth Cemetery, where his memorial is maintained by the entertainment charity, The Grand Order of Water Rats, of whom he was a King Rat[3]. The inscription reads Here sleeps the King of Laughter-Makers. Sleep well, dear heart, until the King of Glory awakens thee.

Dan Leno remains an important figure in the development of comedy in the late 19th century. Along with the likes of similar music hall stars such as Marie Lloyd, Albert Chevalier and George Robey, legendary masters of mirth such as Charlie Chaplin, Buster Keaton and Laurel and Hardy owe a debt to him and the enduring humour from this period.

Dan Leno: Bibliography

Dan Leno, by J. Hickory Wood, Methuen, 1905
The Funniest Man On Earth, by Gyles Brandreth, Hamilton, 1977
Dan Leno: Hys Life, by Dan Leno, Greening & Co, 1899
Northern Music Hall, by G.J. Mellor, Graham, 1970
Harlequinade, by Constance Collier, John Lane, 1929
Fairs, Circuses and Music Halls, by M. Willson Disher, Collins, 1942
British Music Hall, by Ramond Mander and Joe Mitchenson, Studio Vista, 1965
The Melodies Linger On, by W. Macqueen Pope, Allen, 1950
Folksong and Music Hall, by Edward Lee, Routledge & Kegan Paul, 1982
Bransby Williams, by Bransby Williams, Hutchinson, 1954

Dame Gracie Fields (1898–1979)

Dame Gracie Fields (1898–1979) born Grace Stansfield, was an English/Italian singer and comedienne who became one of the greatest stars of both cinema and music hall.

Born over a fish and chip shop owned by her grandmother in Molesworth Street, Rochdale, Lancashire, she made her first stage appearance as a child in 1905. Her two sisters, Edith and Betty, and brother, Tommy, all went on to appear on stage, but Gracie was the most successful. Her professional debut in variety took place at the Rochdale Hippodrome theatre in 1910 and she soon gave up her job in the local cotton mill. She met comedian Archie Pitt and they began working together. Pitt would come to serve as her manager and the two married in 1923. Their first revue in 1915 was called Yes I think so and the two continued to tour Britain together until 1922 in the revue Mr Tower of London. Fields came to major public notice when Mr Tower of London came to the West End. Her career rapidly accelerated from this point with straight dramatic performances and the beginning of a recording career.

One of her most successful productions was at the Alhambra Theatre in 1925. The show, booked by Sir Oswald Stoll, was a major success and toured for ten years. She made the first of ten appearances in Royal Variety Performances in 1928, gaining a devoted following with a mixture of self-deprecating jokes, comic songs and monologues, as well as cheerful "depression-era" songs all presented in a "no-airs-and-graces" northern, working class style. Fields had a great rapport with her audience, which helped her become one of Britain's highest paid performers, playing to sold out theatres across the country. Her most famous song, which became her theme, "Sally," was worked into the title of her first cinema film, Sally in Our Alley (1931), which was a major box office hit. She went on to make several films initially in Britain and later in the United States (for which she was paid a record fee of US$200,000 for four films), despite never enjoying the process of performing without a live audience. Ironically, the final few lines of the song 'Sally' were written by her husband's mistress, and Gracie sang this song at nearly every performance she made from 1931 onwards. The late 1930s saw her popularity peak and she was given many honours: the Order of Officer Sister of St. John of Jerusalem (for charity work), the Commander of the British Empire (CBE) (for services to entertainment) in 1938, and the Freedom of the Borough of Rochdale. She donated her house, "Tower," in London's The Bishop's

Avenue (which she had not much cared for and which she had shared with her husband Archie Pitt and his mistress) to a maternity hospital after the marriage broke down. At the time, she was seeing Irish painter John Flanagan, who she later said that he was the only other person apart from Boris Alperovici (a later husband) who she loved. In 1939, she became seriously ill with cervical cancer. The public sent over 250,000 goodwill messages and she retired to her villa on Capri. After she recovered, she recorded a very special 78 record simply called Gracie's Thanks, in which she thanks the public for the many cards and letters she received whilst in hospital. Fields, accompanied by an RAF orchestra, entertains airmen at their 1939 Christmas party.World War II was declared whilst she was recovering and Fields travelled to France to entertain the troops. In 1940, she married film director Monty Banks, following her divorce from Pitt. However, because Banks remained an Italian citizen and would have been interned in the United Kingdom, she was forced to leave Britain for North America during the war. Although she continued to spend much of her time entertaining troops and otherwise supporting the war effort outside Britain, this led to a fall-off in her popularity at home, where she was portrayed by the press as a traitor and deserter. Nevertheless, she performed many times for Allied troops, travelling as far as the islands of New Guinea, where she received an enthusiastic response from Australian personnel. After the war, Fields continued her career on a less active basis. She began performing in Britain again in 1948 and starred at the 1951 Festival of Britain celebrations. She proved popular once more, though never regaining the status she enjoyed in the 1930s. She continued recording, but made no more films, moving more towards light classical music as popular tastes changed. Although there is some doubt that her British citizenship was ever re-granted after the war[2] (she lost it due to her marriage), she did a great deal of charity work, and established a permanent home on the Isle of Capri, Italy. Monty Banks died in 1950. Fields married Boris Alperovici two years later. After that, she began to work even less, but still sold out theatres even into her seventies. In 1956, Fields played Miss Jane Marple in a US TV production of Agatha Christie's A Murder is Announced (IMDB entry). The production also featured Jessica Tandy and Roger Moore, and predates the Margaret Rutherford films by some five years. In 1978, she opened the Gracie Fields Theatre in Rochdale, Lancashire. It is located next to Oulder Hill Community School. Her final appearance was at the Royal Variety Show at the age of 80, when she sang "Sally" in the finale. In February 1979, she was created a Dame Commander of the British Empire seven months before her death at her home on Capri, aged 81. She is buried in the non-

Catholic cemetery on Capri. Rochdale Boroughwide Cultural Trust holds the Gracie Field Archive.

Gracie Fields: Famous songs

"Sally"
"Sing As We Go"
"Thing-Ummy-Bob (That's Gonna Win The War)"[1]
"The Biggest Aspidistra in the World"
"Only a Glass of Champagne"
"Angels Guard Thee"
"Nuns' Chorus"
"Now Is the Hour"
"The Isle of Capri"
"Walter, Walter, Lead Me to the Altar"
"Christopher Robin is Saying His Prayers"
"Wish Me Luck As You Wave Me Goodbye"
"When I Grow Too Old to Dream"
"If I Knew You Were Coming I'd've Baked A Cake"
"The Twelfth of Never"
"Those Were The Days" -Famously performed live at [The Batley Variety Club] in [1968]

Gracie Fields: Filmography

Sally in our Alley (1931)
Looking on the Bright Side (1932)
This Week of Grace (1933)
Love, Life and Laughter (1933)
Sing as We Go (1934)
Look Up and Laugh (1935)
Queen of Hearts (1936)
The Show Goes On (1937)
We're Going to Be Rich (1938)
Keep Smiling (1938)
Shipyard Sally (1939)
Stage Door Canteen (1943)
Holy Matrimony (1943)
Molly and Me (1945)

Gracie Fields: References

Gracie Fields: A Biography by Joan Moules
Gracie Fields: The Authorised Biography (1995) by David Bret
"Gracie Fields" by Jeffrey Richards (in the Oxfordtionary of National
    Biography)

Vesta Tilley (1864 – 1952)

Vesta Tilley was one of the most famous and commercially successful Musical Hall artistes of her era and was a star of both music hall and pantomime in both England and the US for over thirty years. Born Matilda Powles, in 1864 in Worcester, England; her father was a factory worker who took to the music halls with his own act and as Chairman at the Theatre Royal Gloucester. Tilley first appeared on stage at the age of three-and-a-half when she was billed as "The Great Little Tilley". At the age of six she first peformed in male clothing under the sobriquet "Pocket Sims Reeves", a parody of then-famous opera singer Sims Reeves. Afterwards she would play male roles exclusively and hone her act as a male impersonator extraordinaire saying: "I felt that I could express myself better if I were dressed as a boy". At the age of eleven she debuted in London at the Canterbury Hall under the name she would subsequently become famous with - Vesta Tilley. Tilley is said to have paid meticulous attention to detail when dressing for her shows, taking over an hour to get ready for each performance. She wore men's underclothes and a special padding so as to "re-construct" her figure since the women's underwear of this era was tightly corseted and would have looked strange under men's clothing. Her hair was reasonably long but she wore it plaited into tiny braids and coiled around her head under a wig. Her most recognisable male character was that of the "swell" or the man about town – the smart, middle class, well dressed and polite individual on which the character in her hit song 'Burlington Bertie' was based. She liked to poke fun at men and their vanities and some of her better-known comic numbers included 'Jolly Good Luck to the Girl who Loves a Soldier', 'After the Ball', and 'Strolling Along with Nancy'. Tilley married Walter de Frece, the son of a theatre owner, in London on the sixteenth of August, 1890. By then she was already a famous entertainer, but her marriage also contributed to the blossoming of her career as de Frece was the founder of a chain of music halls called *The Hippodrome* where Tilley would become a regular act. Extremely professional in her preparations, she would spend months working on new character types and new stage numbers. Her stage performances frequently had a slightly mocking humour to them, an aspect of her style which solidified her popularity amongst the British working class, men in particular. As a male impersonator, Tilley played the role of soldiers, sailors, bellhops, policemen - young men in sporting clothes, boaters, stiff collars, morning kit, fancy waistcoats - and full white-tie-and -tails evening dress complete with top hat, gloves and cane. She toured America where she a big success and also moved into Pantomine - playing Principal Boy in such pantomimes as *Dick Whittington*.

Both men and women looked up to Tilley, with women frequently viewing her as a symbol of female independence. Tilley's popularity reached apex during the First World War when both she and her husband ran a large recruitment drive on behalf of the British Army. A large number of other other music-hall stars, did likewise at this juncture but Tilley was probably the most successful of them all. In the guise of characters like "Tommy in the Trench" and "Jack Tar Home from Sea", Tilley sang songs such as "The Army of Today's All Right" and "Jolly Good Luck to the Girl who Loves a Soldier", stage numbers which were credited with swelling the ranks of the army's volunteers. Apparently, young men were sometimes asked to join the army on stage during the course of her shows. As part of her support for the military, Tilley also sold War Bonds and performed in hospitals and were subsequently honoured by the British State for their efforts.   In 1919, her husband Walter de Frece was knighted for his services to the war effort and Tilley received the title of Lady de Frece. Vesta Tilley's last performance was in 1920 at the Coliseum Theatre in London. She was fixty-six years of age by then and both she and her husband retired to Monte Carlo. Tilley returned to England after the the death of her husband in 1935, her autobiography *Recollections of Vesta Tilley* having been published the previous year. Vesta Tilley died in London in 1952, aged 88.

Vesta Tilley: References

Maitland, S. (1986) *Vesta Tilley*; London: Virago

Anew McMaster (1891-

Anew McMaster is considered one of the icons of the Irish "fit-up" or touring theatre tradition. An "archetype" of the nineteenth century touring actor tradition, in many ways McMaster was a throwback to such renowned pre-twentieth century touring artists as the Irish touring actor

Gustavus Vaughan Brooke. McMaster made Ireland his theatre and he spent thirty-five years touring the country. Known simply as Mac, he emerged firmly from the British actor-manager tradition and would also prove one that traditions last representatives. During the course of his working life, McMaster and his travelling theatre witnessed enormous changes and challenges in the nature of theatre, whether it be the emergence of "talking pictures" in the 1920s or the "threat" of television three decades later. One glance at McMaster's own theatrical curriculum vitae is enough to confirm this. His stage beginnings were in such artistes as Julia Neilson and Fred Terry in the lavishly-produced *The Scarlet Pimpernel* while he played the part of James Tyrone in the U.S. National Tour of *Long Day's Journey into Night* towards the very end of his stage career. As with several noted Irish actors whose theatrical oeuvre was forged in the rough halls and damp-ridden schools of pre-war Ireland, McMaster was actually born in Liverpool, England in 1891. His father Andrew was Irish, of Scotch-Presbyterian stock while his mother Alice, who died when Mac was just three-and-a-half, was a Liverpudlian. Relatively little is known of McMaster's own theatre-going experiences as a boy and how his first interest in the theatre was piqued. His father, who was a hard-working businessman involved in shipping seems to have been a distant figure and it may be that it was the search for a sense of "family" or "belonging" that first drew McMaster in the direction of the theatre. What is clear is that McMaster's childhood coincided with the apex of the touring theatre tradition in Britain when great plays could be seen on a regular basis in most English cities. McMaster's involvement in theatre became a lifelong passion and as a young man he set up his own company and moved to Ireland during the Emergency years.

By then, McMaster had already toured Ireland as a jobbing actor for more than two decades as a jobbing actor (often under the pseudonym Martin Dolan) with Irish companies such as the O'Brien Company. Having moved to Ireland, he would carve out a lasting reputation for the quality of his acting company's productions, one which persists in Irish living memory to this very day. MacMaster's primary audience was in Ireland's country towns and his forte was Shakespeare's theatrical oeuvre. His company was mainly composed of young actors and actresses from both Ireland and England and alongside the thirty-three years spent circuiting Ireland, MacMaster's company also toured as far afield as Britain, Malta, Australia and Egypt. The life of a touring actor was a hard one and actors had to be versatile, hardworking and (preferably) healthy so as to last the pace. Actors had to learn quickly and a typical weekly routine would have involved something along the lines of:

Open on the Sunday night, play seven nights a week with as many as five matinees. Close again on the following Sunday and take down (pack) the set; travel to next venue early on that Sunday morning; on stage again that very Monday evening. McMaster relied heavily on his wife Marjorie McMaster, who was the administrative backbone of the company and his children who were also heavily involved in the touring. The company's "bread-and-butter" plays comprised the prescribed Shakespearean texts for that current school year, plays which were often preformed in the local school. When money was scarce, these were the "earners" which ensured the continued survival of McMaster's company through the leaner periods. His reception from the Irish audiences of his day appears to have been the catalyst for McMaster's renowned artistry and drive - as eloquently described by actress Dorothy Primrose once in a BBC interview (see note below):

> I can remember an interminable train journey when [Mac] talked to me about what he said was his favourite way of acting. Touring around in Ireland and playing in the smallest possible towns and villages, in halls and tiny places, where the audience had no idea of how the play was going to finish. I can remember him talking for about twenty minutes when the audiences would shout out encouraging words and give him advice, and with that sunny sort of smile he said he was often tempted to take their advice and wondered how the play would finish up. In the tomb scene in Romeo and Juliet, right at the very end someone cried out in great distress, "O, give her a good shake!"

Anew McMaster: References

Falb, C. *A World Elsewhere: The Stage Career of Anew McMaster.* PhD. Thesis Ohio State University, 1974.
Leahy, J. *"People Must be Amused": Touring Theatre Companies and Travelling Shows in Munster during the Emergency Years,* (M.A.. Drama and Theatre Studies, UCC, 2007.

Note: Quote from a short BBC interview on the touring shows. Cited in Falb, C. *A World Elsewhere: The Stage Career of Anew McMaster.* PhD. Thesis Ohio State University, 1974, 16.

Gertie Gitana (1887-1957)

Gertie Gitana born Gertrude Mary Astbury in Stoke, England in 1887. Her father was a pottery works foreman and her mother was a teacher. Gitana, which is the Italian for "little Gypsy" was involved in music hall and theatre from a young age and was a member of Tomlinson's *Royal Gypsy Children* at the age of four. Her petite form and alleged "Gypsy origins" meant that she was also sometimes billed as "The Staffordshire Cinderella". She made her professional stage debut at the age of eight at *The Tivoli* in Barrow-in-Furness and two years later she played at the *The Argyle* in Birkenhead, near Liverpool. She was just thirteen when she made her first appearance on the London stage and four years later she topped the bill for the first time at *The Ardwick Empire* in Manchester. This Manchester show was her entré to the big-time. She subsequently became a household name and was able to command high wages given that her "name" on the bill-poster would ensure ensure a full house. Her music hall repertoire included such numbers as 'A Schoolgirl's Holiday,' 'When the Harvest Moon is Shining,' 'Silver Bell' and 'You do Look Well in Your Old Dutch Bonnet,' The song 'Nellie Dean,' as written by Henry Armstrong, which she first sang publicly in 1907 became her "signature tune" however, and ensured that her voice made it onto some of the first gramophone recordings – (made on the Jumbo label) ever made in Britain - dating from the period between 1911 and 1913. She became a "Forces' sweetheart" and regularly entertained the war-wounded performing in hospitals and sanatoriums. After the war she made starred in pantomimes such as 'Little Red Riding Hood', and 'Cinderella' and she even had two musical shows which were specially written for her - *Nellie Dean* and *Dear Louise*. She married fellow-artiste Don Ross in 1928, retired a decade later but made a hugely successful come-back ten years later again when she joined other "old timers" in the show *Thanks for the Memory* produced by her husband. She died in January 1957. A London memorial to her - *The Nellie Dean* - at the corner of Dean Street in Soho and encompassing a large collection of her stage memorabilia was a "shrine" to her at one point. Today her stage name "Gertie Gitana" is frequently recalled, often unwittingly, in the London Cockney slang term for a banana – i.e. a Gertie - (Cockney rhyming slang Gertie Gitana = banana).

MAE MACK: A TRIBUTE

When I went to visit Mae Mack at Tobermolina in Oulart, County Wexford, little did I realise what I was letting myself in for. As we sat in her cosy mobile home and stuffed our faces with "dainties", what a treasure trove of information Mae turned out to be. With her amazing memory the list of names which trips off her tongue provides a veritable "Who's Who" of the traveling shows going back way back. She is also the owner of some terrific historical photographs. Not only were Mae and her mother Margaret (Daley) Lyons the first showpeople to meet Vic Loving when she came to Ireland in 1926, but their friendship was an enduring one, one which lasted until Vic's death in 1974.

Mae's own history in the business goes back to when her father Eddie Mack ran a very genteel "Concert party" from the year 1906 onwards. Born Edward McSherry in Ballyboy, County Monaghan, her father did not come from a theatrical family. His background was a religious one and his family were scandalized by his entering what they considered to be a very unsavoury profession!

Eddie's brother John E. Mack joined up and toured for a while, but show business was not for him. Some years later Jack Stanley-Lyons joined the show, and when his sister Margaret "visited" him she liked touring so much that she stayed...later becoming Mrs. Eddie Mack!! Margaret had been born in Cloughjordan, County Tipperary, where her father worked as a headmaster, but it is not on record what her family thought about her traveling way of life!!

Born in 1916, Mae was only about three months old when she was carried on stage as Mrs. Pixton's baby in Jane the *Lady Slavey*. Whilst her two older sisters were at boarding school, Mae continued with her "child parts" such as the renowned Little Willy in *East Lynne*. Some years on, she not only studied but wrote out her own part for *Cry of Conscience*, at the Theatre Royal, Wexford, a fact she is justifiably proud of, seeing as she had not started her "formal" education until the age of eight.

Eddie Mack had a large company of English artists, as very few Irish people toured at that time. Pat McEntee was on the show, having come over from London, before going on to run his own company-, another artist was Lena Lewis. Using hired transport, the company toured the whole thirty-two counties. All aspects of the performances were taken very seriously, this having rubbed off on Mae, whose attention to detail can be seen in her work to this day.

There were eight in the family, but only Mae, her brother Charles and sister Dolly toured-The two sisters did a song and dance act, but Dolly died in 1925.

Having a large family, and due also to the heavy entertainment tax, Eddie stopped touring for a while and got a "steady job" in insurance!!! At the age of fifteen she left school, and when her father returned to the road she went with him and met another member of the company who would become her husband; comedian and accordionist James Hudson. They were married in 1942 and left to join Flay Merth's company in Co. Cork. Mae and Jimmy later went on to form their own show.

One story which Mae recalls happened in the 1940's: "We were travelling along some very narrow roads in Count Leitrim, when the lorries came to a dead stop. In front of us were two men digging a ditch. We looked at them and they gazed back at us, trying to figure out who or what we were. They suddenly started to fill the whole ditch back in, to let us pass by....it wouldn't happen now!!!" she says with a smile…

Mae and Jimmy had two children, Margaret and Monica. When Jimmy died in 1950, Mae being the woman she is 'got on with it' - and having two children to support - continued with the way of life she had been born into, joining Harry and Jimmy McFadden's company that same year. They had a huge tent and as the show moved every couple of days (á la circus) this presented problems. So it was decided to do 'weekly' dates instead.

Amongst other things, Mae's forte is management, and one of the shows which she managed for a summer season was Paddy Dooley's in Ballybunion County Kerry. Following on from this she went into partnership with Mollie Fitzgerald whom Mae had known since childhood, another long-standing friendship. Mae's daughter Monica also performed on the show. She is an accomplished musician/singer, and produces musicals within the area where they now live. Wexford was Mae's 'area'

for touring, and the show crisscrossed the county for several years playing
the many villages and towns which dot it. "They were good to us", says
Mae.   So successful was the alliance between Mae and Mollie that their
company - The Mogodor Players - toured up until the 8th December 1970,
and were the second last show to come off the road...

> Show people were a different kind of people; they had a kind of aura",
> Mae muses...She is right. Mae has a lovely ladylike quality without being
> 'frilly', a wry sense of humour, and still continues to do Trojan work for
> her love of the theatre. She is one of the true "all-rounders"...
> —Vikki Jackson

PARLEY: LANGUAGE OF THE SHOWPEOPLE

Accompanist
A musician, often a pianist, who provides musical support (or *accompaniment*) to singers or comedians.

Acoustics
The quality of the sound in any auditorium.

Act-drop
A cloth or a curtain loered as opposed to drawn, at the end of each act, instead of the front curtain or house curtain.

Arc
Common abbreviation of carbon arc spotlight – widely used for flood-light illumination priot to the invention of the electric bulb.

Are you decent?
This was once a common phrase spoken at the door of the dressing room, the then equivalent of "May I come in?"

Babyspot
A small spotlight used to light limited areas of the stage sharply.

Backcloth/Backdrop
Two terms which describe the same stage feature: a large curtain or canvas painted to represent a particular scene, and suspended from the grid at the rear of the stage.

Ballyhoo
To ballyhoo is to create a spectacular effect, the random swirling of the the stage lights known as the follow-spots.

Barker
A tout employed by circuses, side-shows and other popular entertainments so as to attract an audience through oral advertisements.

Batten sometimes abbreviated to **bat.**
    This is a word with a very old theatrical pedigree and can signify:
1)   A long, narrow piece of squared timber used in stage building or as a support.
2)   a strip of timber attached to the top and/or bottom of a *cloth* to ensure support and a "good hang".
3)   strip lights or border lights (American term) – a row of lanterns placed as footlights.

Beginners
The cue-call "Beginners!", to announce the beginning of a show, is guaranteed to get the actors/actresses adrenalin pumping.

Between engagements
An actors' euphemism for periods of unemployment.

Bill/Billing
Bill is used in a variety of combinations e.g. playbill, hand-bill etc. in theatre advertising.

Blacks
Black curtains used in the theatre.

Black tat
Black waste fabric which finds a variety of theatrical uses, particularly to stop unwanted leak[s of light.

(The) Boards
From the standard sense of "a piece of sawn timber". Wooden platforms supported by vertical poles or bracing in order to form a stage.

(The) Book
Full and accurate version of the script. Also can refer to the promptbook, prompt script or prompt copy.

Boom
Vertical or horizontal wooden spars or beams from to which scenery, equipment, and latterly, lights could be attached.

Booth
Traditionally, booths were makeshift canvas shelters or stalls which could be easily constructed or dismantled. Historically, booths were used in medieval passion and pageant plays and they continue to be used on fairgrounds, markets and in circuses.

Border
A narrow strip of curtain hung behind the proscenium arch to hide lights and equipment.

Box
A term first used in 16th century theatre, referring to a small, private room in a slightly elevated position near the stage.

Box-office
Where the customers pay to enter the theatre. Probably so-called because it was the place from which the (theatre) boxes were originally hired out.

Brace
A device often known as a *stage brace* made of wood or metal which would secure or support. Often a wooden rod attached on one end to the back of a stage *flat*.

Bravo
An exclamation from the audience meaning "very good" or "excellent"

Break a Leg
During that period when the front curtain was brought "up" the crossbeam was supported on two "legs". The more "encores" the cast received, the greater the danger that the heavy curtain would "break a leg".

Bridge
A type of movable platform – usually above the stage -where preparations as relating to lighting and scenery can be performed.

Burlesque
Any type of theatrical performance that could be classed as satirical or mock-heroic comedy
This term made a revival in the mid-late 1800s particularly in America where it was used as designate bouts of political satire set alongside

variety sketches and singing. From the early 1900s onwards burlesque was a word which became increasingly associated with a more "seedy" form of performance, striptease in particular.

Cameo
A brief but very well-acted character part in which an often (well-known) actor might be cast. Sometimes used in theatre and film to denote an *extra.*

Canvas
Piece of strong cloth used in theatre to construct the *flats*; i.e. a piece of canvas stretched over a wooden frame. Ideal for decoration with oil-based paints, and utilized for this purpose by many painters and other artists. *Under canvas* – i.e. "in a tent" – tents as used by Travellers, Fairground Travellers and Circus people.

Carnival
A term which, in the Medieval era, referred to the period prior to Lent. Carnival later came to have a broader meaning signifying any period of festivity. In the modern era the term Carnival has a particular association with street theatre and community theatre in the current era – as relating to largescale events such as the Notting Hill Carnival in Britain and the street theatre of Macnas in Ireland.

Call
The *call* is the traditional name for the order of the order or warning that actors, crew etc. receive to appear for rehearsals, performances, for cues within a show, or to take a bow e.g. the curtain call at the end of a show.

Call boy
A member of the stage crew, frequently somebody who was pensioned off from heavier work, and whose job it was to call the *half*, the *five* (i.e. inform the cast how long they have left to get ready) or to make sure that the actors are in place for their cues.

Catchphrase/catch
Catchphrases referred to particular ("familiar") phrases as associated with certain stand-up comics and as relating to particular music hall artistes.

Chairman
In music hall parlance, the *chairman* had a similar role to the individual known as the *compere* in variety; i.e. the person who is the "master of ceremonies" and who introduces the various acts.

Chinqua
Five

Cloth
Another word for a *backdrop* or the *drops*. This material was usually made of canvas and was generally stretched across the rear of the stage or hung from the *flies*.

Come down (to)
A show comes down when the curtain comes down. i.e. when the show ends.

Comps
An abbreviation of complimentary tickets.

Counterweight system
A system of weights, lines and pulleys which allows heavy pieces of scenery to be raised and lowered.

Cover
A term referring to a particular form of light.
A wash of light which covers a substantial area of the stage.

Dame
A female role in pantomime. This role was frequently traditionally played by a male actor.
This part was often the role of the hero's mother.

DBO
Dead black-out. The abbreviation refers to a point in the play when all of the lights are cut and the theatre is plunged into complete darkness – usually for dramatic effect.

Detail scenery
Small pieces of scenery - usually custom built for the play in question – and which are brought on or removed from the set during the performance or production.

Digs
The lodgings where actors, actresses and variety acts stayed while on tour.

Dim
Decrease the intensity of the light used on stage, usually slowly and gradually. Interestingly, the lighting device known as a *dimmer* could be used either to increase or decrease the lighting intensity.

Dinarii, wedge
Money

Dips
Small pockets or traps in the floor of the stage which contain electrical sockets for use with microphones or lights.

Dock
A space or area where scenery and other stage equipment can be worked on or stored.

Drag
A female impersonator – i.e. a male performer who specializes in female roles.

Dresser
Somebody who helps the actors and actresses get dressed before the performance or between costume changes.

Dui
Two

Extemporize
To ad lib or to improvise.

Falling flaps
Stage flaps, usually hinged, which were important for the swift transformation of scenery, particularly in variety and pantomime. These

scenery flaps were decorated on both sides so that after one side had been shown to an audience during a particular scene, a hinge could be released and a completely new scene would appear.

Farce
A comedy genre which is reliant on improbable plots, slapstick action and unlikely coincidences.

Feed
A variety or musical hall term. Originally it referred to a support actor or "straight man" who supplied the principal comic with cues for his jokes or gags.

Five, (the)
A call (reminder) issued to members of the cast to tell them that there is only five minutes left before the beginning of the show.

Five and nine
The name given to the greasepaint sticks, numbers five and nine.

Flash box
A term used for a container, often a metal box, in which the material used to produce a stage flash - (or an accompanying puff of smoke). Was often used in pantomime.

Flats
Pieces of scenery. In the past, the flats consisted of pieces of canvas stretched over a wooden frame.

Flies
The area above the stage from which the scenery and the lights hang and which are lowered or raised as required.

Flipper
A wooden support for a flat. This is often attached to the flat with hinges.

Floods
Intense lights which can "flood" a large section of the stage with light.

Follow spot
A beam of light which can "follow" the actor/performer when they move around the stage. Often used in variety shows, especially to focus the attention of the audience on a particular singer or performer.

Footlights
A term which refers to lights which are situated downstage or below stage level e.g. low-angle lighting.

Front of house
Those sections of the stage or theatre that are not *onstage* or *backstage* and which are open to the public.

Full up
A reference to the lights being at their very brightest.

Gaff
The word *gaff*, as used in the eighteenth century referred to the "penny shows" that were performed on fairgrounds, travelling shows which generally moved from one fair to another. A century later, a gaff generally referred to any building that was used temporarily for theatrical performances, especially music hall.

Gaffer
Term referring to the person in charge of the theatre, the fairground or the travelling show e.g. the employer or boss.

Gauze
A form of netting or thin cloth which can be decorated like a normal stagecloth but is transparent to light – from either the front or the back. Often used in pantomime for scenes incorporating magic or illusion.

Get-in, get-out (the)
The terms "get in" and "get out" were frequently employed by travelling shows and fit-ups to refer to the efficient shifting of props and scenery from one venue to the next.

Grease-paint
Make-up. Grease was mixed with other oils from an early date as a form of make-up. From the mid-1800s onwards greasepaint increasingly came in the form of numbered sticks.

Half, (the)
A cue-call indicating that there is a half an hour left prior to the beginning of the performance.

Hand
Another word for *stage-hand*. A member of the acting troupe or stage crew who often does the "heavy work", the shifting of scenery for example.

Hand-bill
Referred to more often today as a "flier" – a small advertisement announcing the time and venue of the upcoming performance.

Heads!
A warning cry as emitted by one of the stage crew when something falls from a height – from the flies etc.

Knockabout Comedy
Slapstick comedy or clowning around as typical of certain types of musical hall or
pantomime acts.

Landlady, Theatrical
A stock figure as relating to the early days of the touring shows and the travelling fit-ups. A landlady with whom some of the acting troupe would often lodge.

Leg, Break a
Traditional good luck "greeting" as issued to a fellow-actor or actress who is about to go on stage.

Leg Show
A variety or musical hall act featuring chorus girls or a chorus line who wear costumes designed to show off their legs.

Libretto
The lyrics and text of an opera or musical show.

Lifts
Inserts worn inside an actor's shoes so as to give the make the performer appear taller than he/she actually is.

Lose
To remove a stage prop during the course of a performance, usually as directed by the stage manager e.g. Lose chair! – Remove the chair!
Lose light! – Turn off the light!

Luvvie/Love
An actor or actress who is self-consciously theatrical or camp.

Mark
A mark made on the stage floor to denote the positioning of a particular prop. This mark is frequently indicated by the use of chalk, paint or some form of tape.

Mugging
A performer, frequently a comedian, who exaggerates his facial expressions for dramatic effect.

Naff
Orginally a Parlari word meaning "of poor quality" or of dubious aestethic value.

Nobba
Nine

On the book
The person who works as the prompter during a performance.

Otta
Eight

Padding out
Adding lines or extra dialogue to extend a scene or to make up for the fact that an actor has forgotten a line or missed a cue.

Pancake
A type of make-up, common in the nineteenth century which was water-soluble.

Patter
Rapid speech or the rapid delivery of a speech. Today, the word is frequently used in a pejorative sense with reference to overly-rehearsed or often-quoted speeches or dialogue.

Piano Wire
An "invisible" wire which could hold heavy scenery and was used to *fly* in pieces of scenery.

Pick Up
This refers to a request to an actor/actress to speed up the delivery of their lines or their acting performance generally. To pick up on your cues means to come in on your ques more quickly.

Pierrot
Pierrot is a stock character of mime and Commedia dell'Arte, a French variant of the Italian Commedia dell'Arte character, Pedrolino. His character is usually that of the sad clown, pining for the love of Columbine, who inevitably breaks his heart and leaves him for Harlequin. He is usually depicted as dressed in a loose, white tunic. The primary characteristic of Pierrot's character is his naïveté. He is the naïve and trusting fool who is always the butt of other people's. The Pierrot character also incorporates a trusting character who is is depicted as portrayed as a dreamer, a character who is distant and oblivious to reality. The Pierrot character entered the English harlequinade in the eighteenth century only to fall out of fashion again. He later appeared again as a stock character in many end-of-pier shows of the late nineteenth and early twentieth centuries.

Pit/Orchestra Pit
A lower-level area in front of the stage in older theatres where the band might play their music

Player
Now an "archaic"word as used for an actor or actress. This word first appears in English dictionaries from the fifteenth century onwards.

Pong
Another obsolete word which may have come into theatrical parlance from Romany "pan" to smell, to stink – or through Parlari. Refers to someone who is forced to pad out their lines by ad-libbing or who exaggerates their

acting to lengthen the amount of time they spend on stage, thereby lengthening the duration of the performance in the process.

Principal
Means the leading actor or actress as playing in a particular stage performance. A term that his still used in both theatre and pantomime today.

Prompt/Prompter
To prompt means to remind someone - who has forgotten them - of their lines, as whispered from the edge of the stage. A prompter is the person whose role it is to do the prompting.

Quarter
In "theatrical time" this is twenty minutes before the theatre curtain goes up on a performance/show.

Quatro
Four

Rag
The curtain that is opened and closed in between acts – also referred to as the tableau curtain

Raspberry
As related to the theatrical term – "to get the raspberry" – refers to an actor or actress who is heckled by somebody in the audience who disapproves of them (or the play). Comes from rhyming slang (raspberry tart – fart) and refers to the sound of a "farting" noise.

Repartee
A frequent term as used in variety revues or in comedy which refers to the quick-witted banter or responses between the characters on stage.

Resting
Euphemistic word used to mean that an actor or actress was "in between jobs" or unemployed.

Roll Drop
Stage size canvas – painted both sides and lowered by pulleys – increases the number of available backdrops for various plays

Setta
Seven (number)

Tray
Three

Una
One

Cain and Abel
Table

Letty, Uncle Ned
Bed

Skimisc
drunk

Clobber
Clothes

I'm Afloat
Coat

Strides, Rounds
Trousers

Flasher/Fletcher
Shirt

Toecase, Gillimor
 Shoe

Jimmy
Waistcoat

Mangaree, Mungaree
Food

Peck
Food

Strike (dead)
Bread

Stammer (and stutter)
Butter

Screw, Dek, Lamp
Look

A deko
A look

Maybe, Don't know
Nantee

Cóbh, Hómó, Hómi
Man

Carnish
Meat

Lag
Arrest

Waddler
Duck

Rozzar, Hornee
Guard, Policeman

Shutter
Gate

Wide
Clever

Whinge
Cry

Bald
Ugly

Mosey
go, leave

Rumble
Tell

Lightee
Day

Casa cóbh
Man of the house

Casa mull
Woman of the house

Croaked
Dead

Bevvied
Drunk

Sluice
Urine

Cottiva
bad, dishonest

Bleeder
Knife

Shobi, shovi
shop

Shobi sham, shovi sham
shopkeeper

Drom, Drag
road, way

Glim, glimmer
Light

Stall, Nark
Stop

Ogler, mince
eye

Weed, Congo, Scald
 tea

Bevee casa
pub

Mosey
come, walk

Clobber sham
 tailor

Flash
Show – (e.g. "Flash her chats, shafts"– "Show her legs")

Casa, Karsee
house

Parlari, Parlarey, Lingo
language

Animateur
The straight man who works with a clown in a speaking gag.

Atching
To camp, or to move to the next lot.

Barney
A fight or an argument.

Batts
Shoes.

Belly Box
A cupboard fixed underneath a wagon, between the wheels, where you can store things.

Bevvy
Beer, or by extension a pub or bar.

Bill
A poster.

Bona
"Good", or sometimes 'please'.

Buffer
A performing dog.

Build-up
Putting up the tent.

Caravan
A trailer (in common use).

Chat
A thing. May also refer to the spiel or the "barker"

Chava
A girl (or in very vulgar use, to have sexual intercourse.)

Chavi or **Chafe**
A child.

Chovey, Shovey
An (old) clothes shop, good for clown outfits or cheap wear.

Daybill
Usually a poster which shows the acts in detail, but properly any poster which is put up on the day of the show.

Dik or **Deko**
To look at.

Dinari or **Dollnaries**
Money.

Dobby or Dobby Set
A merry-go-round (q.v.) on which the seats are fixed to the ride's rotating platform. When most seats move with an up-and-down motion the ride is a "galloper." (From "dobbin", familiar name for a horse).

Donah
An older woman.

Dots
The band's sheet music.

Dukkering
Fortune telling.

E. O.
A fairground gambling game.

Feke or **Fake**
A whip (noun,) or as a verb, to make or do something surreptitiously or dishonestly. You can *feke* something to someone by giving it to him secretly. A bad person can *feke* an animal by hitting it.

Flatties
Non-Showpeople or Non-circus people.

Flick-Flack
A backward handspring. See the American term "flip-flaps."

Fun Fair
What in America would be called a "carnival".

Gadge
(Sometimes "gadjo" or "Gorgio" or "gadje") - anyone who isn't a Gypsy.

Gaff
The fairground. Romani for 'town.' In Victorian slang, a show or exhibition, a "penny gaff" was a cheap show or vulgar entertainment. Also, can have the same meaning as in America: the subterfuge by which

a game is rigged or a stunt or trick (including magic tricks) is operated. Another uniquely British meaning is "to mess something up."

Gaffer
A gentleman, or the boss.

Gallery
Traditional circus bleacher seating - ike steps. Low gallery seating has only seat boards and your feet touch the ground. In high gallery seating you put your feet on the board (and sometimes the clothes) of the person below.

Galloper
Merry-go-round (q.v.) of British manufacture, especially one on which most or all seats are horses and most or all have an up-and-down motion.

Grai
A horse.

Heath Robertson
A 'jerry-rigged' cobbled-together repair.

His Gills
One of the names you use when you don't remember a person's real name; 'whatsizname.'

Jal
Romani both for 'to come' and 'to go.'

Jal Orderly
To come or go quickly; to pack up and get on the road smartly and quickly or set up the same way.

Jib
The lingo.

Jogger
To entertain.

Joggerin' Omee
Entertainer, especially a street musician.

Jossers
Non-Showpeople or Non-circus people.

Jugal
A non-performing dog (ones that just hang around.)

Bad
Kativa, Kottiva

Ken
House or office.

Khazie
Toilet, from the Romani for 'door.' Spellings vary widely, sometimes "Carsy" or "Kazy." The term has passed into countrywide use.

Kushti
Nice.

Lacing
The system of eyelets on one edge and rope loops on the other edge of a canvas top which are used to join sections of canvas together. Also the edge of a section of canvas which has either eyelets or hoops, e.g. "pass through the lacing."

Lunge Line
A centrally-fixed rope tied to a horse's head to keep it running in a circle.

Mangiare
Food (for humans or animals), from the Italian for "to eat."

Martin Harvey
Refers to a legendary performer whose chief talent was faking illness to get out of performing.

Merry-Go-Round
One of the oldest amusement rides, a circular platform holding seats usually shaped like horses and almost always accompanied by band-organ music. Also see "roundabout" and "galloper."

Minger
Policeman. Most Romani terms for the trades end in some variant of "-engro.'

Molti, Multi
Very much.

Mr. and Mrs. Wood and All the Little Woods
Empty seats in a house.

Nanti
No, nothing, or don't.

Omi, Homee
A man.

Pal
Friend; Romani for 'brother.'

Palone, Poloni
A young woman.

Panatrope
Recorded music.

Paper House
A performance where most of the patrons came in on free tickets.

Parca, Parker
To pay up.

Parlari
The circus and fairground "in" language. As a verb, to talk.

Parni
Water.

Parni Chat
The gentlemens' toilet. Chat = 'thing.'

Patter
The words used by showpeople or clowns in a speaking act, or the narrative spoken by someone during an exotic act. In general theatrical use, a "patter song" is a song full of intricate rhymes executed as rapidly as diction will allow.

Pig
Applies to any animal with particularly small eyes (even elephants or bears.)

Prad, Prag
A horse.

Pug
A monkey.

Pull-Down
Dismantling the tent.

Rakli
A non-Gypsy girl (Raklo for a boy).

'Recting
Putting up the tent (short for "erecting").

Ring Doors
The curtained-off area behind the artists entrance, made so that the performers can stand in the tent without being seen.

Ring-Door Curtains
The curtains through which the artists enter the ring.

Ring Groom
In the days of horse-drawn circuses there were two sorts of horse grooms: those for the draft horses and those for the ring (show) horses. Nowadays a ring groom is the man who fetches and carries props in the show.

Rokker
To understand. "I rocker the jib" means "I understand the language."

Roller
The special harness used on a Ring Horse by the bareback rider. It has a handle on each side.

Romani
The Gypsy language, from which many Showpeoples' terms and Circus terms derive.

Roundabout
A merry-go-round. Also called "carousel" if the ride is of American or European manufacture, and "galloper" (q.v.) in some cases.

Rum Col
Literally, Romani for 'best friend.' In use, the boss.

Run-In
A short bit done by a clown to fill in a pause. The clown runs in to do something that is not long enough to be an actual act.

Scarper
To run away; to 'burn the lot' or 'pay them off in the dark.' To 'scarper the tober' is to run off without paying the rent.

Shush
To steal.

Slanger or **Slang**
As a noun, the tent.
As a verb, to work, as in "Are you going to slanger today?"

Slap
Makeup.

Spot
An act. A performer's first spot is usually his speciality act, his second spot another type of act.

Stick-and-Rag Show
A low-quality 'mud show.'

Tentmen
Roustabouts.

Tent Master
Boss Canvasman.

Tawni
Small.

Tilt
The Big Top, the "roof" of the tent.

Tober
The circus lot, from the Romani for the road, as in 'on the road.'

Tober Omee (Homee)
Circus owner, or lot manager; the boss.

Toby Clown
Clown who works the road leading to the tober (lot).
Toby Mush
Tramp.

Voltig
From the French or German for flying, the equestrian trick in which the performer jumps on and off the horse, stands, kneels and even dances on the horses back

Wallings
The canvas walls of the tent.

SELECTED REFERENCES

Ashcroft, B. et al. (eds.) (1995) *The Post-Colonial Studies Reader*; London: Routledge

Ashcroft, B. and Ahluwalia, P. (eds.) (1999) *Edward Said;* London: Routledge

Atkinson, P. and Hammersley, M. (eds.) (1992) *Ethnography: Principles in Practice*; London: Routledge

Cannadine, D. (ed.) (1982) *Patricians, Power and Politics in Nineteenth-Century Towns;* UK: Leicester University Press

D'Alton, L. (1938) *Rags and Sticks*; London: Heinemann

Fitzpatrick, D. "Entertainment in Ashford, 1900-1950" in *Ashford and District Historical Journal*, No. 4, July 1995. pp.26-27.)

Fitz-Simon, C. (1983) *The Irish Theatre;* London: Thames and Hudson

Foster, R. (1988) *Modern Ireland 1600-1972*; London: Allen Lane

Harrison, M. (1993) *The Language of Theatre*; Manchester: Carcanet

Harry Tate - http://en.wikipedia.org/wiki/Harry_Tate

Harry Tate (Music Hall Performers) – http://home.clara.net/rfwilmut/musichll/xtate.html

Hayes, Michael (2006) *Irish Travellers: Representations and Realities*; Dublin: Liffey Press

Hewitt, M (eds.) (2001) *Unrespectable Recreations;* Leeds: Leeds Centre for Victorian Studies

Joyce, N. (1985) *Traveller: an Autobiography*; Dublin: Gill and Macmillan

MacLiammóir, M. (1961) *All for Hecuba*; (rev. ed.) Dublin: Progress House

Walton, J.K. (1983) *The English Seaside Resort: A Social History 1750-1914*; UK: Leicester University Press

Some Further Research Sources

For other stories and anecdotes referring to Vic Loving and the Travelling
Shows please refer to the following Irish local history publications:

Days by the Shannon
Charleville Journal
Kilfinane Journal
Castlebridge Co. Wexford Journal